interludes

interludes
linda andersen

a busy woman's invitation to personal and spiritual rest

WATERBROOK
PRESS

INTERLUDES

PUBLISHED BY WATERBROOK PRESS

2375 Telstar Drive, Suite 160

Colorado Springs, Colorado 80920

A division of Random House, Inc.

All Scripture quotations, unless otherwise indicated, are taken from the *Holy Bible,
New International Version*®. NIV®. Copyright © 1973, 1978, 1984 by International
Bible Society. Used by permission of Zondervan Publishing House. All rights reserved.
Scripture quotations marked (KJV) are taken from the *King James Version*. Italics in
Scripture quotations reflect the author's added emphasis.

Details in some anecdotes and stories have been changed to protect the identities
of the persons involved.

ISBN 1-57856-385-2

Library of Congress Cataloging-in-Publication Data

Andersen, Linda, 1940-
    Interludes : a busy woman's invitation to personal and spiritual rest / by Linda
Andersen.— 1st ed.
        p. cm.
    ISBN 1-57856-385-2
    1. Christian women—Religious life. 2. Rest—Religious aspects—Christianity. I. Title.

BV4527 .A485 2001
242'.643—dc21

                                                                            2001017535

Printed in the United States of America

2004

10 9 8 7 6 5 4 3 2

To all women of every age
who find the courage to counter their culture
where it hinders their walk with Christ.

Contents

Acknowledgments

My hat is off to WaterBrook Press, a publishing house honestly and deliberately doing its work as unto the Lord. It has been my privilege and distinct honor to join hands and hearts with its staff on this project.

I owe a deep debt of gratitude to my gifted editor, Traci Mullins of Eclipse Editorial Services, who has a heart as big as Texas. It was my joy and delight to work with her as she brought her impressive package of skills to bear on this manuscript, both enhancing the message as well as clarifying it.

PART I

A Holy Turning

As Jesus and his disciples were on their way, he came to a village where a woman named Martha opened her home to him. She had a sister called Mary, who sat at the Lord's feet listening to what he said. But Martha was distracted by all the preparations that had to be made. She came to him and asked, "Lord, don't you care that my sister has left me to do the work by myself? Tell her to help me!"

"Martha, Martha," the Lord answered, "you are worried and upset about many things, but only one thing is needed. Mary has chosen what is better, and it will not be taken away from her."

LUKE 10:38-42

Reclaim Your Lost Moments

"But Martha was distracted by all the preparations that *had* to be made." Sound familiar?

We Americans have never really known how to take it easy. We've never mastered the art of slowing down. Acceleration is our middle name. Since the foot of the first Pilgrim touched American soil, it has been so. For fear of losing ground, we have pushed westward at such an alarming rate that we now find we are losing anyway: losing relationships, losing the joy of the present moment, and, most of all, losing our way spiritually. The biblical mandate to allow sabbath (periods of rest) into our lives has been trampled in our rush to get ahead.

At one time this rush toward "success" and conquering every obstacle was primarily male. But in the past thirty years, women, too, have entered and run the race. And now neither men nor women believe we have permission to live a rested life. Nor do we know how. We no longer recognize the principles of restedness and balance that infuse Scripture; rather, we have published our own bibles that tell us how to get *more* done *faster.*

Frankly, it hasn't worked, has it? Many of us, both men and women, have hungry hearts, impoverished souls, and depleted physical reserves. What is God's solution to our often self-imposed overload? His answer is plain, and it is simple, but it is not easy. *Rest. Pause. Stop. Wait. Listen.* Discover and celebrate the God-designed life of both work and rest: life with time enough to be sick, time enough to enjoy friends, time for mates and children, time for vocation and avocation, time for dreaming. And time for God. For there *is,* for every one of us, whether or not we believe it, *time enough.*

I believe women, in particular, need pillows of time to call our own—safety nets of uncluttered moments and even hours we can ink onto our calendars and look forward to. I'm convinced that time to relax and open our spirits to God is *the* great missing element in women's lives today. My fervent hope is that this book will provide the encouragement and practical help you need to reclaim the joyful, rested, and balanced life that is your birthright as a woman of God.

> *"People are discovering that the din of daily life can drown out what one ancient spiritual sage called a still, small voice."*
>
> —TIMOTHY JONES

Time to rest. "An impossible dream," we sigh. Just a wild idea to toss aside. Simply "not doable." I'm afraid we as American women are better than most at forgetting to enjoy life along the way. We expertly dodge or perpetually postpone rest and balance, choosing instead the accumulation of things or titles or others' approval. Many times this is unintentional, but often it's simply the way we choose to live. As a result, many women are now feeling the pinch of the trap and are beginning to make courageous and often misunderstood choices to *really* live. To embrace time for rest, for play, for art, for love, for God. Life, as designed by our culture, has imploded on some, and they are rebelling.

"I was endlessly serving and never being nourished," says one woman whose life became unbalanced as she strove to be wife, mother, and busy church worker. "I now know that God wants me to be renewed. Relaxation helps me face life better equipped in all ways. I now know the difference between serving and *over*serving. Because of my human frailty, I need renewal if I'm to have anything for anyone else.

"Over the years, I've been told how talented I am. This praise made me seek to do too many things at once. And because I didn't discipline myself and keep activities in perspective, my life soon needed an overhaul."

How about you? Does your life need an overhaul—or at least a minor tune-up? Are you ready for a little righteous rebellion against a cultural code that perpetually works against your God-instilled desire for rest and balance? Are you open to a holy turning from all that is now to all that can be?

A woman who is the sole proprietor of her own business recently told me, "It has finally dawned on me that probably no one—not my clients, not my culture, not even my friends and family who love me—are going to walk up to me and say, 'You deserve a break today!' That's just not how the world we live in operates. I am *always* 'on call,' and I'm realizing that no amount of mere wishing for rest and peace is going to stop the phone from ringing and the assignments from piling up and the ex-pectations of others from growing. If I want a manageable, joyful, and rested life (and I do!), then I'm going to have to lis-ten to my deepest self and my God instead of all those other voices. I'm going to have to learn that it's okay—in fact, it's crucial—to make room for my own soul, to say no to a ca-cophony of distractions, and to deliberately choose interludes of rest and communion with God that restore my personal bal-ance and enrich my spiritual life. I've sacrificed so many precious moments to that god called productivity. I value hard work, and I'm happy with my professional and personal accomplishments. But I know in the core of my being that there is more to life than what I've been experiencing. I am ready to reclaim what I've lost and, with God's loving direction, build on a different foundation."

Rest is the precursor of productivity. It is also work's sweet reward. We simply cannot work well unless we rest. God has graciously woven rest into the very fabric of his plan for our work. In the Old Testament covenant God made with his chosen people Israel, he made a great promise: "Before all your people I will do wonders never before done in any nation in all the world. The people you live among will see how awesome is the work that I, the LORD, will do for you" (Exodus 34:10). He proceeded to tell Moses all that he required from the people under the terms of this covenant. There was a lot of action involved in being faithful to God. But one thing he made crystal clear was the value of rest. "Six days you shall labor," he said, "but on the seventh day you shall rest; even during the plowing season and harvest you must rest" (Exodus 34:21). Every farmer knows that there is no busier time than plowing time or harvest time. But God says to rest *even then,* right in the middle of our busiest times.

In my view, this call to the discipline of rest is nothing new, unless it is new to the women of America. It harks back to the Garden of Eden where God visited daily with Adam in the garden. I believe the inner yearning we feel to savor peaceful moments is the very call of Christ himself: "Come to me, all you who are weary and burdened, and I will give you rest"

(Matthew 11:28). For a woman to habitually ignore this call on her soul is to walk past who she is and who God is. Needless to say, so much is missed!

But a woman's soul is insistent. Even when the call of duty threatens to drown out the cry for personal and spiritual renewal, she hears it and responds, if ever so briefly. She cannot allow her soul to be servant to duty alone. For a woman to choose to rest before everything is "done" is an affirmation that none of us is indispensable and that God will ultimately provide. So, in the very middle of work to be done, we can choose rest as an act of faith.

> *"Spiritual disciplines are ways to truth, stepping stones from our furious activity into God's calm and peace. When we have crossed over on the stepping stones, we escape into the life of grace."*
>
> —EMILIE GRIFFIN

This book is all about how to find rest and the joy that comes with it—to discover sacred cutaways and exquisite moments, even hours, that exist right now in each of our lives. They are already there! They have just been lost in the jumble. But there is every reason to believe that we can recover those lost moments, those tiny personal holidays that invigorate us for our tasks and refurnish our souls with joy. At such times, we hand our empty cups to God, eager for refilling.

And a woman needs that filling. *Because* her life is busy, she desperately needs room for her heart and mind to relax—to stretch out and to daydream. Precisely *because* most of us are on duty twenty-four hours a day, we must intentionally devise times of personal refreshment. In planned interludes away from the constant onslaught of demands, we are made aware of our mortality and of the magnificent eternal presence of a living God. If there were ever a time to reinvent life as we live it, surely it is now. Why not *relish* the simple rituals of everyday life instead of postponing our enjoyment to a one-week block called vacation (from which we usually need another vacation to recover!)? Why not *feast* at the banquet of life instead of merely snatching at morsels?

By the very act of relaxing, women will find their hearts leaning expectantly toward God, listening for his voice, admiring his handiwork in new ways, and developing a longed-for intimacy with him. Without this warmth and intimacy with God, even the most devoted religious life can become barren and joyless. Without close fellowship with God, we are like arid deserts, having forsaken the very fountainhead of life. We run through life, while he waits by the well. He reaches out, but we race past, just out of touch, escaping the very embrace and long, cold drink of refreshment we so long to experience.

This book is about *making room* in our lives to become fully devoted followers of Christ—followers with light in our eyes and a bounce in our step. It's about becoming intimately acquainted with the vast heart of God and stopping long enough to acknowledge his power in the lightning and his voice in the wind. It's about taking delight in the bounty he provides and allowing a thankful spirit to emerge from the morass of our overburdened lives. In his kindness, God intends for us to live balanced, rested, joyful lives of ongoing fellowship and celebration with him and with others. He has given us *the* Sabbath as well as little sabbaths along the way. But so often we crash past them in our rush to keep up. Life need not be this way. We have more choices than we think.

As one wife and mother of four says, "Whenever I go at a breakneck speed, I can't hear God. And breakneck is something I do to myself. It's something I can change." Another working mother of two adds, "Time with my God is a sweet-smelling savor, but I seldom have it due to my failure to plan. But when a new day comes so do new choices."

In myriad ways God reveals himself to us, but most particularly when we rest or stop, when we come to a complete halt and take off our running shoes. Resting moments allow us to regain perspective on our lives and renew our energy to embrace the future. Mountains become molehills. The impossible suddenly becomes manageable. And God becomes our Friend above all friends. So it is with great excitement and anticipation that I urge women to simply watch the raindrops on the windowpane, to touch the roses, and to admire the clouds. Because I know a Friend awaits.

My prayer is that this book will also become a friend to you, leading you into the innumerable delights of personal and spiritual rest. As you read, give yourself permission to rediscover the God who loves you, just as you are, and who is more excited than you are at the prospect of a closer relationship. He does not call you to rest merely so you can work better or harder, but because it is your birthright as a child of a loving Creator who delights in watching his children at play just as we do.

"I never need to be encouraged to work," says the same mother of four—three teens and a baby! "But I do need encouragement to rest—to believe it's not only okay, but it's a gracious provision of God for me. At this time of my very busy life, I have to make rest a part of my workday, or I just keep going and never stop."

This book—your personal book of interludes—is your invitation to stop. It's a lot like your favorite candy bar: something to be savored. It's not a book to rush into, but to move through slowly with a sense of expectation. You might want to have a chapter with lunch or save it for your day's dessert, dipping in right before bedtime. I encourage you to read the chapters in part 1 slowly and thoroughly, as they will help you establish the right foundation for enjoying the restful interludes to come. Then give yourself permission and freedom to choose the interlude that's right for you on any given day. The suggested time frames are provided to help you choose according to whatever is going on in your day or week. Once you pick an interlude, read through it, but most of all, go on to *experience* it. In the process, you'll undoubtedly discover ways and means to have many other kinds of personal interludes. You may want to jot those ideas in the back of the book to remind yourself that there are many wonderful moments to be had for the taking.

Interludes is a book of joys, which I offer with joy, having slowed down my own gallop to an unhurried canter and having become enthralled with the uncanny and irresistible presence of God. Why would I ever want to run haphazardly down the middle of a highway again when I can stroll along a rose-edged path?

"There remains, then, a Sabbath-rest for the people of God; for anyone who enters God's rest also rests from his own work, just as God did from his. Let us, therefore, make every effort to enter that rest" (Hebrews 4:9-11).

Sabbath (a period of rest) is good. Sabbath is right. Sabbath is a gift from almighty God to us, his children, who seem to insist on not receiving it. Written all over Scripture is an invitation to your weary heart. God rested. Christ rested. The Jewish people were required not only to rest but also to hold long, jubilant celebrations regularly. For days they feasted and danced and laughed and sang.

Doesn't it sound good to "sip" at life rather than fast-forwarding your way through it? Perhaps you have written everything on your calendar except rest and play. And perhaps that's the key: *Write it in.* Begin to establish your "resting turf" by writing it *in ink* on the calendar. Write in half an hour or an hour. Set aside a half-day or a whole day. Recapture the time in your life before it slips through your fingers like so many grains of sand. Do it *before* events collide. Do it now. With those highly personal appointments on your calendar, you will have no need to explain when requests come. You are simply "not able to." "It won't work" for you. For the sake of your soul, your body, and your loved ones, you are not able to, because you are busy being restored yourself.

So, my friend, go ahead. Lay aside the ordinary, and get ready for the extraordinary. May you fully experience the God who is there in the midst of your restful moments.

Lord of life, I am so excited! Here I am, standing nervously on the exhilarating edge of significant change. I mean really significant change. I've tried all the usual stuff (as you know). I've followed the crowd and done a lot of good things and had them turn out acceptably well. But more and more I'm asking, Why? What have I gained? And, more important, what I have lost?

I am so ready to step into new waters. I don't know where the stream will take me, but I am carried along by the hope that there is hope.

So, God, pluck me out of the jet stream where I'm going nowhere at the speed of sound, and set my feet on the pathway to joy. I'm standing here more than ready for you to take over. Take everything out of my hands that simply doesn't belong there, then fill them with whatever you want to. My life feels

like a giant, overstuffed toy, too heavy to carry any longer.
I've done it my way… Now it's your turn.

---

*"With his last bit of strength He cried with a loud
voice in the dark—so powerful that it freed the soul
from the flesh, rang out of the darkness and lost itself
in the furthermost ends of the earth. More than nineteen hundred years have passed and men have inten-
sified the tumult of their lives that they may drown
out that cry. But in the fog and smoke of our cities, in
the darkness ever more profound where men light the
fires of their wretchedness, that prodigious cry of joy
and of liberation still summons every one of us."*

—GIOVANNI PAPINI

Be still, and know that I am God.

Center Your Heart

If you are a novice at resting but an expert at busy, your initial interludes may be a lot like meeting a stranger: tentative, awkward, slightly uncomfortable. Perhaps your life has been lived to both margins of the page without any white space, and you are a stranger to a productive yet restful life. If so, be encouraged, for you're in a perfect place to begin, even though you may not know what to do, where to go, or what to do when you get there.

And when you do begin, there are some things to consider as you accept the invitation, from Christ himself, to embrace restful interludes.

> *"While our lives are full, they seem somehow less than they could be. They resemble a page crammed with too much type—and the margins get narrower all the time."*
>
> —Timothy Jones

First, please relax about the whole matter. Rest isn't yet another thing to do, another commitment to work into your schedule. Rather, as you begin to incorporate small times of rest into your life, you'll clarify your thinking about what really is important and find the unimportant and the unnecessary slipping away quite naturally, even effortlessly.

But be patient. A rested life doesn't usually occur overnight. You'll need time to transition. You'll need time to reposition your heart and announce to your soul that restful interludes are important. Don't expect too much too fast; just let the shift in priorities happen gradually.

"I used to have guilt when I stopped," says one wife, mother, and singer. "But when I discovered that Jesus himself said to rest, that changed. Now there's no guilt. I'm stopping for the sake of myself, my family, and my relationship with God. I'm learning that God values my heart above my to do list. When I allow myself interludes, the Holy Spirit is free to reign and do his job as counselor, comforter, and chief bottle washer in my life."

As you turn this corner in your own life, inviting God to lead you into fresh, green pastures and beside calm waters, you may realize that all of a sudden you simply feel exhausted. You may have run so fast for so long that your soul has never had time to catch up with your body. You may need to take naps for a week before you do anything else. That's as it should be. Sleep is just one of God's many gifts to us. Sleeping in the presence of God is not rude, you know. Take your time—what's the hurry? You will find your way, and it will be *your* unique way to weave tranquil moments into your days.

When you feel ready, you may still notice a listlessness when you try to rest, or daydream, or read, or take a slow ramble through the park. Don't be surprised in the least, for rambling is decidedly un-American. Don't work at it too hard. Shrug your shoulders and just begin. You'll calm down sooner than you think.

At first you will probably also encounter some uneasy thoughts like *This isn't getting me anywhere.* Or *What will I have to show for this? I'm not producing!* Such statements will be absolutely true...and this truth will become delightful. As you learn to embrace refreshing interludes, you will find yourself caring less about production and more about really living a well-rounded life, one edged with the lace of everyday joys. You will learn that rest is an integral part of a balanced life, and then you will feel uncomfortable only when you *aren't* enjoying regular times apart. Although a rested body and a joyful heart ultimately produce work of a higher caliber, you will come to the point where you aren't resting just so you can produce better and faster; rather, you rest because of the simple joy of it—and because God invites you to.

"One day I was able to pay a visit to a horse stable where some of the race horses were worth thousands of dollars. Their stalls were completely padded to guard against any infection from little scrapes and bumps. How much more should we as God's women guard our inner chambers!"

—SHARON HOFFMAN

During your initial quiet interludes, you may feel as if you should be studying the Bible, reading inspirational books, or at least praying—something generally understood and accepted as "spiritual." Of course you may do these things, but you are also free to simply be quiet and let God speak to you. May I suggest that resting quietly is, by itself, an act of trustful worship? May I declare it an act of surrender and openness to what God wants to say to your welcoming mind and heart?

You may want a small notebook and pencil on hand so you can write down any impressions you feel may be from God. But even this is not necessary. It is enough to simply rest—to "abide"—to meet God in the sanctuary of your heart where he prepares a perpetual feast for the two of you.

This journey toward a rested and fruitful life is good and necessary for us all if we are to experience the promise of Christ himself, who proclaimed, "I have come that they may have life, and have it to the full" (John 10:10). If we are always and utterly responsible to others and for multiple tasks, to the neglect of our own souls, then we invite a feebleness of spirit and a shriveling of our capacity for lasting spiritual vitality. To neglect regular rest and reflection is to invite heart disease of the kind no one in our frenetic culture is talking about.

But quiet interludes will change all that. And you are now, at long last, about to begin.

 God! It seems as if I have been jogging past my life for so long. Is there really any hope for me? I'm used to fast. I know how to hurry. I'm an expert at planning and rushing and squeezing in and adding. But frankly, God, I don't know much about slow and what's-your-hurry kind of living. Even slowing down a little bit scares me a lot. What will I do with the time? And what will people who notice think of me?

Oh, but this invitation appeals to me. I want it. Way down deep, I'm sick and tired of designing my life to look like everyone else's. I'm just plain weary. But I'm going to need all the help I can get. So that's why I'm here. And that's why I'm telling you. Is that okay?

Quite honestly, Lord, I don't know of anyone else to tell. I just don't think there is anyone who would really understand. I love it that you made me and know me inside and out. I don't have to explain myself to you or rationalize any of this. It's so freeing to just speak plainly, without masquerading. And somehow I sense that you've already been waiting for me at the SLOW sign for a long time. If that's the case, here I am. And I have a feeling I'm in for the best ride of my life.

> *"Too many well-intentioned people are*
> *so preoccupied with the clatter of effort*
> *to do something FOR God, that they*
> *don't hear Him asking if He might*
> *do something THROUGH them."*

—THOMAS R. KELLY

The apostles gathered around Jesus and reported to him all they had done and taught. Then, because so many people were coming and going that they did not even have a chance to eat, he said to them, "Come with me by yourselves to a quiet place and get some rest." So they went away by themselves in a boat to a solitary place.

MARK 6:30-32

Choose a Place to Call Your Own

Most of your life you share with someone else: children, a husband, coworkers, friends. You share your space and you share your life. And it's good and it's right and it's okay—most of the time. But in the hiding places of your heart, if you listen, you'll hear a need to have a place to call your own.

From the time we are children, it seems, we want a place that belongs to us alone. Signs reading "No boys allowed" and "No girls allowed" proclaim our urge for privacy. A longing for solitude wells up inside most of us regularly, no matter how occupied or diverted we are. In fact, the busier we are, the more insistent God's invitation to "come away" (Song of Solomon 2:10, KJV).

So, then, where will you find your own place of quietness and reverie? Perhaps finding the answer begins with a personal inquiry into who you are and what you love. What kinds of places soothe you? What environs relax you? Why not take a mental stroll through the things and places you love, recalling what it is about the scenes, the scents, the colors that soothe and refresh you. With that knowledge alone you will have begun your journey to the lost land of restfulness and repose.

"When we create an atmosphere that is pleasing to our eyes and beautiful in our sight, we are replenished by being there. As we are replenished, we are energized to enjoy life and all it holds."

—TERRY WILLITS

Do you love flowers? Then you will love flower gardens and florist shops. Do you love books? Then you will naturally be drawn to spend long hours in libraries or bookstores. Do trees enchant you? Then it's the woods for you. Are you attracted to water? Then a brook or pond or lake or wide-open sea will beckon you. And what about plants? Paintings? Fragrances? Sunshine? Music? Where are these delights quickly found in your life?

What are your favorite scenes, and where are they? I take a country road to a flowing river and stroll the riverwalk. Sometimes my car is my special place, as I roll down a country road with my favorite music playing. Other times, it's my porch swing. I sometimes linger long and happily in libraries and secondhand bookshops. I actually keep a list of my favorite places in case I forget. What a delightful task to make such a list!

Think… Where will *you* be compelled to linger? There you will meet yourself and your God.

> *"My special place is a small brook in a green glade, a circle of quiet from which there is no visible sign of human beings."*
> —MADELINE L'ENGLE

A place of rest will, of necessity, be a private place—a sanctuary set apart for uncommon use. Anne Morrow Lindbergh put it so well when she said she was "diminished" in the company of too many others and "recreated" in solitude. For the most part, an ordinary place won't do. It should have special meaning, a kind of set-apartness—even if it's only a favorite chair in a nook that you visit regularly.

My daughter, when she was small, chose as her special spot a chairlike opening at the foot of a giant maple tree. There, on her walk home from school, Kelly paused to review her day and anticipate her evening. There, she was halfway between school and home. No expectations. No demands. She was free to simply be herself—a necessary and nourishing freedom for a soul of any age. You, too, will need to find your own endearing and private place to begin remembering who you really are, to consider why you are here, and to make room for God to visit your heart.

If you like, your private place can be small and near. Start by looking around your home. Is there a corner in your bedroom? A space under the stairs? An attic? A deck? A porch? Writing in *The Not So Big House,* architectural designer Sarah Susanka says, "Whenever you tinker in the garage or retreat to a sewing room, you're expressing the need for a place of your own. Perhaps the search for the essence of a place—a room of one's own—has contributed to the scale of houses today: More and more rooms are planned in an attempt to create distance and separation. But all that's necessary to create a place for yourself is a very small area—truly just big enough for one. Such a place should encourage you to be yourself."

Susanka's own private place is a small attic, accessible by a ship's ladder. She writes and she meditates there. My sister-in-law simply uses a chaise lounge in her bedroom. In my home, though small by today's standards, I have several places to retreat alone. Each area is multipurpose, but each has a place for me.

My porch is secluded and partially hidden by an apple orchard; it is the most pleasant of places to spend a quiet hour. It has only a suspended swing, two wicker chairs, and a small table to hold refreshments. There I hear the sounds of the morning, yawning itself awake, and there I sit after dark to say good-bye to the day.

In my bedroom is a small writing desk, overlooking the

orchard and a flower garden. It, too, is a place of respite used by no one else. There I journal, and there I write notes to those I love.

My studio, in its soft yellows and greens, is a garden of color and a pleasant place to write or do handcrafts.

Our tiny attic, papered in floral designs, is a devotional center for me in the morning.

Even the most familiar chair can become an exotic place, a comforting haven, and an island of peace for your tranquil moments. In your chair, you can paint a portrait of joy by gathering around you items that please and nourish you. Savoring your own nook is all a part of caring for your soul and replenishing your strength. The painting near my own special chair reminds me of the treasured friend who gave it to me. Nearby, the cane-shaped stick covered with ivy serves as a greeting from the lovely lady who once used it for a walking stick. A vase of silk flowers is a "hello" from the one who gave it with love when our home was brand-new. The pen in my hand is a warm handshake across the miles from the giver.

You can find other solitary places away from home: a library, a bench in a park, a biking path, a coffee shop, a bookstore, a scenic overlook where you can park your car and simply gaze. In fact, your car can serve as a portable sanctuary. Wherever you choose to "come away," relish the soul peace that is beyond understanding and that only God can give. You are not supposed to be at peace in such a world as this, but you can be. And such peace is a gift from God.

A place of your own is out there. You can find it or make it. And it will add joy of the finest kind to your life. You will know you have found a place of value to you if it fosters a bit of day-dreaming and a spurt of senseless joy just to be there. It will be as if you have, at long last, found or been found by an uncommon joy and creativity. The important thing is to find a spot where you can experience the companionship of God and hear your own heart beating with his.

The place or places you choose for your interludes should invite inspiring thoughts and easy reverie and contemplation. Places of inspiration often contain these elements: music, crackling flames, rushing water, color, flowers, animals, visual beauty, scenic splendor. Our all-wise, creative God had us in mind when he lovingly provided all we need for restful and abundant living. And I think it must grieve him to see so many of us running at full tilt, bypassing simple joys. God has laid out a banquet of sensory pleasures in his creation, and he invites us to this feast of life. He has pulled out the chair for us to be seated. Fellowship with us is his greatest pleasure.

So let the feasting begin! Find your places of solitude and refreshment and open the windows of your heart to the God who has been lonesome for you—the real, quieted, centered you.

Lord, you've said in your Word that if I ask you, and if I seek, and if I knock, you will open doors for me that I can't open on my own. So I'm asking, seeking, and knocking, because this place-of-my-own thing sounds out-of-sight wonderful to me! I could let my thoughts wander and relax my heart. Maybe I could regather some of my scatteredness and become more whole. It could be a trysting place for you and me.

But it has been so long since we've really seen each other, I don't know if we'll recognize each other. You say you never change, though, so I'll probably know you by your love. And if it's all right with you, Lord, I think I'll just need to be quiet in this newly discovered hideaway and bask in the pleasure of your company. I know my words are pretty jumbled right now and my vision is undoubtedly distorted. But I'm tired of trying so hard…at everything. Let me just be here…now… with you…and in the quietness of the moment let my heart untangle itself.

I never thought I had permission, somehow, or time to find a place of my own to just be…with you. But what is life if it doesn't include spending some of my time in places where I can just plain unravel? I'm ready. I'll see you there.

"A closed door, a comfy chair,
a view through a window—
maybe that's all a hideout requires."

—SUSAN ALLEN TOTH

A furious squall came up, and the waves broke over the boat, so that it was nearly swamped. Jesus was in the stern, sleeping on a cushion.

MARK 4:37-38

Simply Be Still

We do not always need to be *doing* something. Sometimes, we just need to sit down…breathe deeply…and do a little nothing at all. We all have to practice just "being" instead of "doing," for a little bit every day, or we get sucked into the whirlwind of activity and we disappear.

> *"Even Jesus slipped away from the noisy crowds to be quiet and alone before his Father."*
>
> —TERRY WILLITS

There are times when all of us want to be left alone. Not only that, but we *need* a block of time when no one can find us, see us, call us, or even recognize us. We want, for a brief time at least, to slip into a trench coat and slouch hat and dark glasses and move quietly into the shadows of life. We want to become untouchable, unreachable, inaccessible, removed from the fanfare. And that's okay.

Sometimes our need to be alone can be met in a small way—a stroll around the block, a few deep breaths and stretches between activities. On other occasions we need more time to simply be ourselves: unguarded, authentic, and deeply human.

When you do find a bit of time to be still, take advantage of the opportunity *right where you are.* Look around you, and decide how you can make the most of this jeweled moment of solitude. If you're at work, try putting your feet up and closing your eyes in the break room. Are you at home? Lie down with cucumber slices on your eyes while the baby naps, or sit on some steps and watch the lazy dance of the clouds. Are you alone and near a bike? Jump on it and let the wind muss your hair.

On my way home from a tiring weekend of ministry, I stopped the car at a rest stop and simply walked beside a wood with a cool drink in my hand. The weekend had been intense, and I had no muscles left even to smile. I needed to "simply be still"—to exist with no agenda whatsoever. I needed to feed on the substantial riches of solitude, if only for a few moments.

"If you want a simpler life, you have to learn to make simplifying choices—choices that involve words like no and not now."

—THOMAS KINKADE

A library is usually a good place to simply be still. It asks no questions, makes no demands, and often offers cushioned chairs and a view.

A ride in the car or on a bike or even on a horse, or a walk after dark with your favorite music can accomplish a world of good for a busy soul.

A short reverie beside a body of water can soothe your heart in a twinkling.

Your own bedroom may offer respite, and you can lie down with your feet propped on a mountain of pillows and close your eyes.

There are nooks for solitude almost everywhere if you're looking for them. We dined in a home just last night that was in the center of a city, yet it offered a wonderful still spot on a vine-covered porch overlooking a serene golf course.

In *Cross Creek,* Marjorie Kinnan Rawlings writes, "I don't understand how anyone can live without some small place of enchantment to turn to." For her, her old farmhouse, Cross Creek in the Florida Everglades, was spellbinding.

And if you are looking, you will surely find or make some place for yourself to simply be still—a place to let your mind wander and your heart slow down and your hands lie quietly in your lap. You will find a place and a way to put your feet up or your head down: a place to tuck away in your memory where you can return, again and again, not because you must, but because you may.

"God reminds me *why* I need to rest," says a busy mother of four. "Just to be with him. Not so much so I can work more or harder, but just so we can enjoy each other.

I see it this way: My husband is wonderful and does so much right, but if he only kept the grass mowed or the mortgage paid and never wanted to simply be with me, I would be shortchanged. I know God wants me to simply be with him regularly. It's as though he whispers, "Won't you just come and sit down and rest with me?"

Go, then, my friend, to a tiny place of sanctuary and know what it is to be unfettered and unencumbered, to be free to be entirely yourself before God with the world at your back. Embrace the necklace of moments and let them guard and protect your soul for the minutes and hours to come.

If you are a beginner, these small intervals of rest may seem like an eternity. If you are practiced, they will be your favorite pastime. "You will inhale happiness with the air you breathe," as John Stuart Mill wrote, "without dwelling on it or thinking about it."

Lord, I can hardly believe you slept during a storm! If I were there, I would probably be straining every last muscle to do whatever I could to keep the boat steady and the water out. I would be desperately engaged in fighting against the elements. But you slept.

Let me think about this: You knew that your Father was in complete control and nothing would happen unless he planned it. And you knew if he planned it, it would be transformed into good somehow. Because you *knew* your

Father, you could rest. You knew he would call you into service when he was ready and if he needed your help.

Okay. There's something in that for me. I think I'm seeing that right in the middle of the storms of life—right there—I need to continue to nurture a rested heart and body. I need to be "on call" to you, but trusting and resting.

Well, then, you will need to make me over because rested I'm not. But I want to be. And I do know you're happy about that desire. But I have to say, this new approach to my life feels awkward; I'm afraid of what it all might mean. I suppose that's natural, considering the way I've lived. To be still is like going to a foreign country without any idea of what I'll see or what will happen to me once I get there. I'll step off the plane…and then what?

So I have to place all my fears in your hands, God. You're the tour guide; I'm your passenger. So here goes: My new plan is no plan. I'm willing to simply be still so you can speak to me and lead me somewhere from here.

"With your calming hand, help me to stop running from you. Soothe the fever that causes me to act like someone who is spiritually delirious."

—SAINT AUGUSTINE

PART II

Interludes

Yet the LORD longs to be gracious to you;
he rises to show you compassion.

ISAIAH 30:18

Begin by Letting Go

Once you have centered your heart and thought about some places that reinvigorate you, you are ready to take your first steps into a slowed-down kind of life that makes room for all kinds of wondrous possibilities.

As you enter your first restful interlude, begin by letting go of your concerns, one by one, in this simple way: Name them. The apostle Peter encourages us to "cast all your anxiety on [God] *because he cares for you*" (1 Peter 5:7). So picture yourself laying each concern, one by one, into the open hands of a caring God. Give them to him, believing he is more than capable of taking care of them not only for these brief moments, but for all time.

Next, take a few moments to collect yourself. Breathe deeply. Purposefully shut out all the voices calling for your attention. Let go of the false belief that your world *cannot* get along without you for even a few moments.

Now enter your personal interlude fully, with your whole heart. Even if you have only a few minutes of breathing and letting go of your cares, that interlude can be a resting place for your soul. When you enter rest with both your body and your soul, you enter a kind of holy of holies where your friendship with God will flourish and expand as you become more intimately acquainted with him and more assured of his love.

> *"Spirituality does demand attention, mindfulness, regularity and devotion. It asks for some small measure of withdrawal from a world set up to ignore soul."*
>
> —THOMAS MOORE

Your interlude can be wordless, or it may flow into prayer. You may find you are so needy once you actually *stop* rushing about that all you can say is "God!" Be assured: That is enough. God hears. He cares. And he can better minister to your soul as you make a friend of silence and learn that prayer is not one-way chattering but the communion of human heart to divine heart.

Give yourself unconditional permission not to produce during your chosen time apart. Rather, give this time as a lavish offering to God and allow *him* to decide how to use it to create in you a new heart and renew a right spirit within you.

Realize that you probably won't experience complete rest each time you "come away," but in making interludes a regular part of your life, you will be "becoming" rested in increasing measure. You will be learning to enter into what author

Richard Foster calls "the rhythm of the spirit." Whereas most of what you encounter during the day subtracts peace from you, this time set apart will *add* peace, counterbalancing the many subtractions.

As the ears of your soul become accustomed to moments of quietness and rest, you will, most surely, hear the whisper of God reminding you of his loving presence, mighty power, and all-sufficient love. God is the seeker of your heart; he eagerly rises to meet you the moment your heart turns toward him. And whenever, wherever you decide to make a place for him, he is there. And it is all about him.

Here I am, Lord. I don't feel very spiritual or very unwound or very anything. But here I am. I so want to become the kind of person who knows how to live a relaxed yet fruitful life. Do I really begin by simply slowing down and just listening to my heart?

I'm embarrassed, God—ashamed, even—of how long it's been since I've really stopped long enough to commune with you. I feel like a stranger talking to a stranger. But I know you will change all that if I just begin. And I'll even shut my mouth so you can talk to me when I get used to this resting stuff. I'll just sit here now. Waiting to see if it's true: Will you rise to meet me here? I know I need you to. I long to get to know you better.

So, as I said, here I am: warts and all. I have a long list of things I need to let go of: worries, plans, what-ifs, and whys. I wouldn't bother you, but I know you're big enough…and I know you want to share my life and my concerns. So here I am, Lord…beginning.

"My soul is fed and medicined
with goodness from your hand."

—SAINT AUGUSTINE

Peace I leave with you; my peace I give you.
I do not give to you as the world gives.

JOHN 14:27

Fast from Noise

You long for quiet…for a space of time where no noise is heard…no music even…no talking and no motors and no rings and no buzzers. You've heard it all and sometimes all at once, and your ears are full of listening and glutted with sound. For these ten minutes, then, you will choose to fast, to abstain from distracting and unpleasant and jarring noises. You will even fast from soothing music. For only in a deep quietness will you recognize how much sound you have been absorbing. Too much.

"The more time you spend with God in quiet solitude, the better you will hear his voice guiding you and directing you in times of busyness and noise."

—STORMIE OMARTIAN

During this interlude, you will leave behind the Walkman, and the radio, and the television, and the computer, and the VCR, and the washing machine, and even the hum of the car. Unplug, shut, close, turn off everything you can that distracts.

Perhaps in one of your chosen places you can stop your ears for a while, and close your eyes, and be still long enough to hear both your heart and the quiet voice of the Lord.

The absence of noise is a prescription for peace that costs nothing except a little time and choice and discipline. You may actually find the absence of noise jarring because you are so much with it and it is so much with you. But just let the peace in. Doing so will be a good thing and may whet your appetite for more.

Consider a "silent night" if you find yourself alone for a while. First, shut off everything that makes noise. Then simply sit or lie down or work a puzzle or do something you haven't done in a long time.

Fast from noise by leaving the radio and CDs off when you're driving.

Consider having a family quiet time every so often: when no one can speak, when nothing electronic is used, and when phones are forbidden. Once in a while, everyone should have access to only his or her own thoughts.

Walk into the woods, and then simply stand still, absorbing the loud silence of the old trees.

Design a quiet interlude whenever you can. Don't answer phones or doorbells or requests from family members or friends who are simply used to you being on call.

You live in a very noisy world, and though you are used to it, noise affects you and robs you of more than you realize. Neutralize the noise with a fast. Often. Rob the world's din of its power to annoy you and cause floating anxiety. You are in control of many of the noisemakers. And know that God can reach your heart so much more quickly when you listen…when your world stops for a few moments and your soul is quiet.

Stop then, for this time, and discover the silvery silence that opens a gentle pathway to the heart.

God, it is so good…so really good to just shut off everything and take a deep breath. It's just you and me and a quiet slice of time to call our own. Why is it that prayer comes more easily? Why is it that I hear you whisper to my heart? "Because it's quiet," you say.

Of course there's all the "noise" in my mind, but even that seems to settle down when the outside noises are gone. I think I'm over-stimulated and under-quieted, don't you, Lord? It's time to stop talking now, and I will.

What is this sound of silence…this provocative parenthesis…this resounding and resplendent quiet? Where has it been? And will it come again? Can a quiet like this become my friend? Will I actually grow to love it?

The questions and answers waltz delightedly together through my silence, and I know I must have begun to enter your rest. Stay close to me, Lord, in this strange and holy hush.

"My Father, I will quiet my soul now
and enter its 'sanctuary' with you."

—SAINT AUGUSTINE

In the heavens he has pitched a tent for the sun,
which is like a bridegroom coming forth from his pavilion,
like a champion rejoicing to run his course.
It rises at one end of the heavens
and makes its circuit to the other;
nothing is hidden from its heat.

PSALM 19:4-6

Greet the Dawn

You've decided to greet the dawn. It's very early, and no one is around. Just you and God. And he is such very good company.

You rose early on purpose, knowing that by starting slowly and quietly you could move with grace into the day, leaving trails of peace in your wake. You also sensed that to greet the day was to meet the One who created time itself.

There! His masterful brushstroke draws liquid layers of gold and red across the hushed horizon in sweeping, broad bands. They are brash, giddy—color upon color emblazoned wide across the changing sky.

There, in the pale dusting of clouds, you see the breath of God, the Life-Giver—the One who gave you life and who sustains it even now. It is an enchanting moment to catch with your eyes and store away in your heart.

Looking around, you see more and more of him—there in the black-tree specters laid dark against the crimson-sky canvas. They are his plantings, these trees: Gargantuan and gawky, they reach skinny arms toward his nourishing light and his quenching rains—as do you.

Only moments have passed, and yet the canvas continues to be splashed with color after exuberant color: divine preparation for the coming day.

In these timeless moments, you are enveloped in a watchful, peaceful expectancy. You don't pray because you don't need to. Words would get in the way of this silent communion with the Creator of all. Side by side and heart to heart with the God of the universe, you sense that to speak would profane the holy hush. To move would be a kind of desecration.

> *"At sunrise, rekindle your spirit—nothing more."*
>
> —VICTORIA MAGAZINE

Silence stands guard on these brief, predawn moments, and you relish the quiet, confident that God has spoken in the sky and compelled your soul into restful trust.

And now! The faithful emblem rises, moving with slow and graceful resolve over the purplish hills. As a babe to its mother, the yearning earth seems to turn gratefully toward the warmth and light of this new dawning.

Even the horizon stands at respectful attention as the great, blazing medallion rises from its sleep. A changing of the guard:

from moon to sun. And from somewhere deep within, your heart cries, "My God, my God, you have *not* forsaken me!"

Because some days are merely gray, you receive today as a golden gift, and savor it as it opens wide to you.

First comes the light…and *such* a light! This kind of light scatters darkness in sky and in soul! The bright-hot fire of a new day pours out of heaven and spills into your deepest being.

Your gift of hours has been opened. "Today" has arrived. You wonder about these hours. Will someone rub hard and uninvited into your life today? Will there ever really be peace on earth and good will toward men? Will you laugh or cry today? You welcome both…in faith.

There is a comforting goodness in rising early—in being a silent watchman of the morning. It has been a fine and a wondrous thing to be witness to the Creator's celestial art. And it's not as if it's over. Oh no. Not ever. It's as if God himself links arms with you and enters your day as fully as you enter it.

You decide it is a good and a necessary thing to greet the dawn. It is a reminder that God will never leave you—never stop rising to meet you. He will never hang a "closed" sign on his door. For the sun is his letter in the sky, and the Cross his seal on the envelope.

"God made two great lights—the greater light to govern the day and the lesser light to govern the night. He also made the stars. God set them in the expanse of the sky to give light on the earth, to govern the day and the night, and to separate light from darkness. And God saw that it was good. And there was evening, and there was morning" (Genesis 1:16-19).

My God, I am simply stunned. The sun shouts your name—it whispers your constant presence! Since the beginning of time it has done so. It makes my spirit kneel. It humbles me. Frankly, I am blown away by your majesty.

God…would you take my too-often-listless and complacent spirit and remodel it? Would you take charge of the myriad wants and wishes that threaten to do me in? Here's my heart: Go ahead and change it, just as you change the night to day. Take your eraser to all my yesterdays, and write anything you want to on my today.

Remind me that even as the sun stands as life-giving guardian over all your earth, you stand guard over me. May dawn never be "just a sunrise" again, but a perpetual and comforting reminder that you are here…in bright and faithful watchfulness.

---

*"Living artfully might require something
as simple as pausing. The vessel in which
soul-making takes place is an inner container
scooped out by reflection and wonder."*

—THOMAS MOORE

The day is yours, and yours also the night;
you established the sun and moon.

PSALM 74:16

Savor a Sunset

At sunset, imagine…

A red-gold medallion hovers tentatively near the rim of the lake, and red ribbons of light shimmer over silver, silky water. Waves, keen and sharp, slap the shoreline, and happy child voices rise and fall on the evening air. Each moment is a new movement of earth, sky, sun, moon. Another day moves stealthily into night entirely without permission. You resist the urge to preserve, to capture, and to rescue this day from oblivion and yourself from all the changes tomorrow may bring. You simply savor the moment.

At sunset…

The sun becomes a looming half circle, lowering into the blue-gray envelope of night: prepared for bed. It stops noiselessly, leaving a blanket of scarlet shadows in the wake of its retreat. Now day—now night. Evening and morning. So little in-between time to consider—to ponder the day and its various and multicolored pleasures and messages.

"A slash of blue—a sweep of gray—some scarlet patches on the way—compose an evening sky."

—EMILY DICKINSON

At sunset...

Cool winds catch at hair playfully, whip hats off heads and set them spinning across the grass. A day recedes, just out of grasp: sweet plum of a day to be tasted and relished—at least in memory.

At sunset...

You say good night to the bright rim of sun: ripe, hot, deep fire of God, warming the heart and rearranging the soul. Holy fire, stealing away worry and care and exchanging them for a languid, lingering peace. Sun! Great carefree globe playing across the sky, pouring acres of golden nuggets across satiny water.

At sunset...

You are given this portrait in the sky to savor. It is a gift given every night, and with it comes permission, a gentle urging, to embrace it entirely and let the hushed moments nudge your soul toward night and rest.

At sunset...

God's glory is reflected on the mirror of the sky. It is a tantalizing peep into the storehouses of the Almighty daykeeper. You bask in the presence of a God who continually weaves himself into the kaleidoscope of all such savory moments. You are enveloped in his glory; you do not even move for fear of jarring placid thoughts.

At sunset…

You treasure the jewel of the moment…finger it…sigh with satisfaction. It's a moment when time stands still and you see God in all his glorious beauty. And you worship at his footstool.

Holy God, I can almost touch your face when I see a sunset. May this wonder of your creation never grow commonplace to me. May it be an arrow pointing directly to you so I can stand in awe. For you know how much I need to look up, to see beyond my current circumstances even while learning to live serenely in the present.

Let the sunset's light be your smile and its rays your arms big enough to hold all the earth…including me. Let its beauty melt away every care of my heart and fill my soul with peace. Let its silent majesty whisper of eternity in the glory of your presence. And let its nightly display give me divine permission to rest…more and longer and better until the end of my days.

"The only begotten Son who is now embraced in the depths of the Father is the one who declares to your soul or mine, the beauty of God. And He will speak to us in silence, from His Spirit to ours, in words that cannot be uttered."

—SAINT AUGUSTINE

My lover has gone down to his garden,
to the beds of spices,
to browse in the gardens
and to gather lilies.

<small>SONG OF SONGS 6:2</small>

Admire a Garden

In a garden, in the cool of this day, choose to walk alone. Like any garden, the one you have chosen requires nurturing and watering and weeding and, finally, admiring and harvesting. It is the admiring you will concentrate on for now. The gardener (perhaps you!) has lovingly tended every plant, and they have become, over time, personal friends.

> *"When I go into my garden before anyone is awake, I go for the time being into perfect happiness. The fair face of every flower salutes me with a silent joy that fills me with infinite content."*
>
> —CELIA THAXTER

During your "admiration walk," look only for good in this garden. Touch the dewy roses, smell the musky gardenias, smile at the jolly pansies, and take joy in the kaleidoscope of color, the variety of textures. Breathe deeply the haunting and sensuous fragrances.

Imagine the flowers as they were born: They began from mere seeds. Let the miracle of growth bewitch and bedazzle you and point you to the Creator who breathed beauty and life into these seeds. Become like a little child: Allow yourself to be overcome with wonder and delight at things you usually either take for granted or brush by in your hurry.

If possible, choose several from among the most beautiful blooms, selecting a fragrant bouquet for your bedside table so it can sweeten your dreams.

Be playful and tuck a flower behind your ear. Nobody is looking! Braid a garland of daisies and wear it for fun, or give it to a child. You can *always* be grown up, but it takes courage and faith to be childlike.

A quiet garden is a private place where whimsical thoughts and latent dreams can bloom. Most of us leave no time and make no place for dreaming, yet great inventions and lasting art and brilliant innovations all begin with dreams. Robert Frost had to farm in order to eat, but his enduring poetry trickled out as he sat dreaming on his front porch and observing the countryside.

Human life began in a garden, and God himself walked through it with Adam in the cool of the day. Is it any wonder we are drawn to do the same? A garden is ripe with messages from God. The astonishing beauty of just one rose brings praise to our lips and dumbstruck humility to our hearts. We can't make a rose. Not now. Not ever.

But then, we don't need to, for God has already done it. And that is enough.

Lord, when I look at these flowers, they seem like tiny, heavenly explosions of your exquisite and creative heart: bursts of beauty from the heights of heaven. Are they? Is more of this what's ahead for me? Is it a taste, at least? I'm glad I took the time for this.

Now that I think of it, you've given so many things to me that aren't…well, essential to life. Or are they? To live without beauty would reduce my time here to mere functionality. I look at this lush garden and wonder at both the liberal and lavish extravagance of your creating and the joy it must have given you. The colors are bold and shimmering here, soft as a baby's breath there. Not a single bloom is exactly like another. Like people. You didn't have to make gardens so beautiful… All flowers could have been the same. But it seems you flung a giddy and showy sampling of heaven down to us for no other reason than to increase our joy!

Thank you, Lord, for the sermon in a garden.

"We all need beauty as well as bread."

—JOHN MUIR

It is good to praise the LORD
and make music to your name, O Most High,
to proclaim your love in the morning
and your faithfulness at night,
to the music of the ten-stringed lyre
and the melody of the harp.

PSALM 92:1-3

Appreciate Music

Is there an instrument you love to play? Then play! Is there a song you love to sing? Then sing! Even if you only sing in the car or the shower, sing and be glad! Do you love the music that others make? Then take time to be alone with your special music and lean into it, really listening to the words, absorbing the melodies and rhythms and letting them pillow your thoughts, if only for a little while.

A dark room is a marvelous stage for music and you. With the lights off or low, or with a single candle burning, you can hear every single note, feel every shift of rhythm, catch the meaning of each word, and be enriched and filled. Daylight and its varied distractions have a way of diluting even the most beautiful music. There are too many competing voices calling for your attention. But in the dark—or at least with your eyes closed—music stands alone, on a pedestal, and each note sparkles like a diamond against the darkness.

"I've always found that so much of life—writing, painting, mothering—falls into place when we address our own, quiet centers."

—NANCY LINDEMEYER

Music can either complement your mood or set it. When you're blue and don't want to be, gladdening music will catch your mood and run headlong into sunny skies with it, dispersing it to the winds. When you're lighthearted and want to celebrate it, choose music that puts an extra bounce in your step and brings a smile to your lips. When waves of anguish roll over your soul, even then—perhaps especially then—music of pathos and exquisite expression can be the best possible companion.

Who are your favorite artists? Collect their work. Where do you most love to sing? Go there often. Find music that is compelling, uplifting, inspiring, stirring. Some songs will always remind you of an event and bring back memories you love. Play those songs often. Other music is silly and fun and helps you be a child. Indulge yourself.

Have you had enough of words? Then listen to instrumental music. Do some songs speak the language of your heart fluently? Keep them nearby. Does some music inspire worship and stir a praising heart? Never be without it.

Music is a gift from God not to be ignored. It is a friend to the heart that longs for rest and release.

_____

God, music does something radical with my heart. The right song says what I want to say—what I can't always put into words. Music helps me unfold, from the inside out. I can feel myself getting closer to the real essence of myself. Not only that, I'm drawn to you. Whatever it is that music does, let it happen. I'm ready.

I remember a song, Lord, from my childhood. It goes something like this: "I sing because I'm happy, I sing because I'm free...." I guess I sing for all sorts of reasons. And I listen to all kinds of music for all kinds of reasons. O God, you use music so well to soothe me and inspire me. What could I possibly do without it?

Keep talking to me through music, Lord. And most of all, use music to help renew a right spirit within me. Thank you, from the bottom of my restless and ragged heart.

_____

> *"Who first created music? God the Composer:*
> *God the Musician."*
>
> —EDITH SCHAEFFER

But I have stilled and quieted my soul;
like a weaned child with its mother,
like a weaned child is my soul within me.

PSALM 131:2

Just Relax and Read

You may be waiting for something or someone. Read. You may
have a slice of time before something else happens. Read. You
may need to rest just a little before beginning something.
Read. You may simply choose to stop in the middle of a day
full of back-to-back activity and insert some personal solace. If
so, read.

Chaise lounges have not lost their appeal as a solitary place
for one. If you have one, or have another chair you love, by all
means choose a book or a magazine and sink happily into the
world of words. Personally, I find it best to have a book of inspirational "shorts" for brief interludes such as this—a book of
real-life stories that will have a positive impact and quickly lift
my spirits. Many such books are available, and you may already
have some on a shelf. Reading about the heroic or inspiring acts
of others has a way of moving us beyond our personal concerns
into the realm of the spirit.

And have you thought of reading your personal journal? An old one, I mean. If you have been a journaler like me, pick a journal from long ago and read a page or two. You'll be instantly taken to the time in which you wrote. You'll even recall the emotions of that moment. Chances are you'll immediately regain some perspective and be reminded of either how a problem was solved or how it disappeared altogether. Often, reading a journal page is an instant reminder of both God's faithful intervention in situations and your own personal growth over time.

Spend your reading moments with a clear glass filled with a delectable drink. Just any old glass won't do. The simple act of pouring a colorful and delicious drink over a mound of ice cubes reminds your spirit that you are worthy of special attention, and…it garnishes your reading moments ahead. Preparing a delightful drink in a lovely container is a kind of "salute" to yourself. It's a small act by itself, but so filled with meaning when done regularly.

"I think most of us look at personal delights as somewhere between minimally important and borderline immoral. We like them, but we're not sure we ought to. We seldom give them a high priority when other demands are competing for our attention. Nevertheless, the soul feeds on simple joys and withers without them."

—VICTORIA MORAN

Yesterday, I stopped on my walk to pick a nosegay of multi-colored flowers. They now sit on my desk in a small crystal vase: deep purple, soft coral, golden yellow, deep amber, and ocean blue. They rest happily, and I am charmed by their presence. So small an act, so big a result. And a reading moment, however short, offers the same possibility for joy.

Beauty shops are good places for short reading time. Doctors' offices are custom-made. Long rides are rich times for dipping in and out of a book or magazine that's been calling your name.

And if your reading moments are to truly refresh and strengthen your soul, you must not choose reading full of push and pull. No time management or "how to be perfect" kind of material will work. During this interlude, refuse to read anything that demands or commands or insists or produces unfounded guilt. No...for a soul must walk away from the insistent demands of even some great books that are better saved for another time.

Finally, there is a way to read when you are relaxing. It is called *slow* reading. Rather than race through or skim, try reading at a leisurely pace, digesting each word or phrase and letting it sink in. When you read something that particularly delights or impresses you, stop. Put the book down for a moment and linger over the impression. Let it wander through your head and settle in your heart. Simply rest and reflect.

I have found that reading interludes can even invite miracle moments. They have the power to transform and encourage and strengthen your spirit, inform your mind, and even energize your body.

For many years I have read in ten-minute time frames. Some years I read as many as one hundred books, but that is not my goal. It's simply happened as I've enjoyed myself along the way.

Read, then, and enjoy yourself today.

Lord, thank you for all the choices I have when it comes to reading materials. Thank you for the libraries and the bookstores and all the other places I can find books and magazines to match my every mood. Thank you for your wonderful Book, the Bible, that offers endless delights to my hungry heart.

Be with me as I select what I read, and be my companion as I read. Be about your work of speaking to my heart and mending my spirit and educating and stretching my mind. Filter whatever doesn't belong or will hinder me in my relationship with you and others. Store deep within me whatever I will need today or on a future day. Separate the good from the bad, the best from second best, so I won't waste time on what isn't truly useful and enriching. Challenge my thoughts so they won't be set in cement. Jostle my opinions so I won't become arrogant. Help me recognize pure truth, assimilate it, and then stand upon it so I won't follow every new "truth" that comes along. Enliven my thoughts so they don't become sterile and uninteresting. Fill me up with your wisdom and love.

Lord, with you at my side and in my heart, this tiny reading time becomes a private and carefree sabbath.

"We are God's vessels for pouring out his love, but if we are empty we will have nothing to offer others."

—TERRY WILLITS

This is the day the LORD has made;
let us rejoice and be glad in it.

PSALM 118:24

Notice
Serendipity

The dictionary defines *serendipity* as an "accidental, unsought-for discovery." I would add to that definition a *surprise...* something that makes your eyes light up and your heart skip a beat. The ability to spot serendipity is something you may have lost on your path to adulthood, but something you can easily recover. The key is to *notice serendipity when it occurs* instead of racing past the magic.

Serendipity is just around the corners of our lives looking for a chance to happen. A smile from across the room...a rainbow splashing the sky...an unexpected kiss...a thank-you note in the mail...a refund we didn't expect...more in our bank account than we thought we had...a chance meeting with an old friend...a helpful stranger just when we need something...the discovery of a collector's piece we've been looking for, for months.

Serendipity is everywhere when our eyes and hearts are open. And it is God's gift to delight our hearts.

"From the time we were small kids, my parents encouraged my brothers, my sister and me to take pleasure in those sweet and simple moments that can pop up on any old day, those moments that are sometimes spontaneous, and never over orchestrated."

—John Hadamuscin

So move with anticipation into this day! Be on the lookout for the marvelous surprises ahead! An attitude of expectancy can change a day—or a year—or even a lifetime.

As you prepare for the day, get ready to be alert. To look. To listen. Then, during the hours to come, expect positive surprises and unexpected blessings. You cannot make serendipity happen, but you can recognize it when it does and accept the joy with gratitude. Someone calls you just to say she's thinking about you, a gentleman opens a door for you, a waitress remembers your favorite food, a friend drops off a homemade pie, a child remembers to pick up his clothes, a familiar Bible verse leaps off the page and penetrates your soul. Serendipity! Cause for gladness of heart…reason to smile…means to "vacation" your spirit. A way to live.

Watch a three-year-old and you will see continuous serendipity through every hour of every day. A child doesn't run past a caterpillar: She or he stops, touches, and delights in the discovery. It doesn't matter where the child was headed: The destination changes depending on the surprise of the moment. Children simply move through their days without a Day-Timer or a plan, from one serendipity to another. Is it any wonder three-year-olds are, by and large, immune to depression? And who's to say we can't recover some of the same simple joy if we are, after all, but little girls at heart? Surely it's worth a try.

So go into your day with wide eyes and a childlike heart, eagerly anticipating what might be just around the corner. If you do, you will discover and uncover what may have been there all along.

Lord…just thinking about possible surprises and unplanned joys ties a rainbow around my day. Really! Frankly, I'm kind of tired of being a grownup all the time. I'm ready to tap-dance through my life a little more, and let serendipity happen. I'm tired of planned predictability…of things happening only when they're "supposed" to…of time frames and objectives and goals that leave no room for real life to happen.

Oh, I suppose I'll need to keep planning to some extent, but here's the difference, Lord: I want you to break in with your delights, your plans, your surprises. I need not become more rigid and rigorous but more placid and pliable. I want to leave room for "maybe" and "so what?" and "why not?" and "let's go!"

There's not much question in my mind, Lord: I need to stop trying to be my own "day planner" and leave room for serendipity to happen.

So let's go, Lord! I'm ready. As someone has said, "Some days, I am simply partial to the joys of living."

"I am sure that He whose mercies are new every morning and fresh every evening brings into every day of my life a new surprise, and makes in every experience a new disclosure of His love, sweetens gladness with gratitude, and sorrow with comfort."

—LYMAN ABBOTT

He also made the stars. God set them in the expanse of the sky to give light on the earth, to govern the day and the night, and to separate light from darkness.

GENESIS 1:16-17

Gaze at the Stars

Pick a starry night to simply stare at the heavens…a night that's clear and not too cool so you can be comfortable under heaven's canopy. If you live in a city, look out a window or stand on a rooftop. If you're in the country, take a walk outside, or sit on some steps and prepare for the show.

After a few moments, notice how small you feel…how small you are! Notice also how really small your particular concerns are when set against the backdrop of so vast a universe, so vast an array of stars twinkling in front of you. Sense the magnitude first of the seen and unseen galaxies…and then of the God who made them all. Let it register that such a huge God became a mere man in Jesus Christ, making a way for you to spend eternity with him. Consider the unimaginable power and love of a God who can create a universe and yet chooses to dwell intimately in your heart. Let the starry host tell its story to your heart, and be reminded of the truth that a God so magnificent concerns himself with *you*—deeply, intimately.

"Ascend in your soul toward the place where we may drink as if from a pure and clear spring, from the source of Love."

—SAINT AUGUSTINE

Somehow, on a starry night, it is easy to talk with God, for he seems so near. When it's dark, and everything but the stars has disappeared, it is as if you are standing face to face—heart to heart—with the Creator of all. It feels easier, on a starry night, to gather up your concerns, and even your dreams, and lift them into hands so capable and so sure. You *know* you can rest secure because he will handle them with utmost care.

In the deep quiet of a starlit night, it becomes easy to remember that earthlife is not all there is, easy to look forward to a promised forever. The burned toast pales in significance. The recent sorrow and the straying child are put in perspective. These will not last forever. You will. God *is*—forever.

Watch the night unfurl like a jeweled cape across the sky, and your thoughts will change. Night thoughts are different from day thoughts...and often closer to ultimate reality. Hear the songs of the night. Let them play across your heart in treble clef and soften the hard places of your day.

For surely God abides among his starry host in a way we cannot tell, but only sense. Draw close, then, to God, and he will draw close to you.

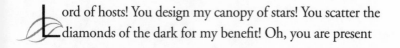

ord of hosts! You design my canopy of stars! You scatter the diamonds of the dark for my benefit! Oh, you are present in the day, but somehow more present at night. There's nothing between us then. It's as if I'm on your doorstep knocking, as if you answer the door and say, "Come in." And then we dine!

Lord, what were you thinking when you spread the tapestry of starlight across the sky? Did you anticipate the delight of your people, who would watch it and wonder? Did you know that the very mystery of stars and outer space would entice our hearts toward you? Did you write your twinkling message of care in the night sky so we wouldn't forget you?

"You alone are the LORD. You made the heavens, even the highest heavens, and all their starry host, the earth and all that is on it, the seas and all that is in them. You give life to everything, and the multitudes of heaven worship you" (Nehemiah 9:6).

The message pulsates across the universe: My God is alive!

"When we behold the Lord, we bask in the warmth
of his presence. Worship and adoration,
praise and thanksgiving, well up
from the inner sanctuary of the soul."

—Richard Foster

I will heal my people and will let them enjoy abundant peace and security.

JEREMIAH 33:6

Gather the Jewels of Summer

It's summer, and gauzy clouds chase each other across the sky in a celestial game of hide and seek. Butterflies glide over lush grasses and form a living mosaic. All of nature seems to be busy in a kind of relaxed motion.

Lest summer disappear too quickly, and lest you miss it altogether, take this handful of moments and allow your mind to dwell on the delights of the season. Let your mind idle for this little while, knowing you will be better for it. Find a place to rest: an easy chair, a garden bench, a walkway beside the water, and welcome the tranquillity of summer. Simply hand yourself over to the ministrations of a loving God who knows how to communicate through his creation.

Open your senses to the colors, the smells, the textures so unique to summer. Relax your heart and take glad notice of everything around you: a silvery cobweb, a shimmering leaf, the fragrant grass and splendid blooms, the silken water. Because you're still and observant, notice a hummingbird as he noses his way into bunches of red geraniums. Listen to the thrumming of his wings and laugh at his busy little body. Bask in the velvet blue of the sensuous, summer sky reaching down to enfold the earth in a breathless embrace and realize that summer is a time to do what comes naturally. The season invites you to be a little more spontaneous, to fly a kite, to laugh with children, to run barefooted, to sing in a gentle rain.

"In the center of each woman's heart is a rose, newly opened."
VICTORIA MAGAZINE

Open yourself to the exquisite pleasures of summer and find yourself bedazzled by what you see when you're really looking. Oh, how the season of summer mothers you—spoils you. On an early summer day, you are blissfully sure that life will always be like this: gold sun on green leaf, pillowy cloud on blue blanket of sky, and flowers upon flowers…a vivacious new season dancing through the doors of spring.

For a time, let your mind drift to old and forgotten dreams. Open your heart like a child and believe again that your dreams can come true. Ask what first step you want to take and let your heart form a prayer around it.

During these stolen summer moments, away from duty and as carefree as the warbling wrens in the trees, look up and beyond and further down the road. Embrace faith and possibilities, and believe in yourself and in your God, who can do far more than you would ever dare to think or dream. Let summer court your soul and captivate your heart.

A tryst with summer will enlarge your appreciation of the small things and broaden your vision of the future. It will bring you face to face with the God who lovingly shares your daily life all year long. All you need do is watch, and look, and gather the jewels of summer into yourself so that you can sift through them in deepest winter.

Though you cannot hold this day, this season, in your hands, you can carry its golden moments in your heart. And you can listen to its message, and know without a doubt that after every winter will come another summer. For hope lies gift-wrapped in this kind of day.

God, most of the time I don't notice the little things…like hummingbirds…around me. Yet summer is so full of little and big things to see and do and watch and enjoy! All this lush beauty just makes me want to throw my head back and laugh out loud into the sky! Your presence is obvious wherever I look! I feel as if you're standing next to me, and behind me, and in front of me, and above and below me at the same time. On a day like this, your presence is irresistible everywhere I go.

I'm just in kindergarten when it comes to interludes like this. But how I love the learning process! To stop and listen and really engage myself with nature takes my breath away and turns my knees turn to water.

Thank you, Lord, for the many joys of summer and for inviting me to revisit my dreams and begin to hope again.

---

*"My living Father, each time I encounter you
in a fresh new way I feel as though I'm rediscovering
a part of myself that was lost, or dead."*

—SAINT AUGUSTINE

The heavens declare the glory of God;
the skies proclaim the work of his hands.

PSALM 19:1

Observe an
Autumn Morn

Call on your powers of observation today and look at what's happening outside. The season is changing, and for these few moments you will welcome it and see it and hear what it has to say. Walk, sit, or even drive, but find a front-row seat for this personal performance and sink your whole heart into the experience, while I tell you of an autumn I remember…

The days must have swept right around the corner of August and into September when I wasn't looking. As I opened the screen door that special morning, an apple-cheeked sun sprayed shafts of melted gold across the sky, and I squinted up at honking geese silhouetted against cotton-candy clouds. The grass, at rest now, wore shimmering silver beads. Our kitten scampered and tumbled after a crisp, brown leaf on the lawn.

Toward evening, I found time to slip out of the house, and a snappy breeze met me on the porch. I snuggled deeper into my light jacket and ignored the goose bumps, while casting a maternal eye at my bed of zinnias. When had those lush petals begun to droop? And who had painted their tips brown?

I was getting cold, so I jogged down the road that slices our hill in two, scaring a squirrel snacking at the base of a maple. "Gathering nuts already?" I called as he disappeared into the tree.

Ahead, a field of crunchy cornstalks waited to be harvested. My breath turned white and hung suspended in the air. When I spied a huge pile of pumpkins in a neighbor's garden, I began to get the message: It was fall. Suddenly, I was wrapped in her cloak. A regal queen, fall. With all of nature as her kingdom, she steals upon the world and stuns her subjects with her majestic robes of every hue.

I retraced my steps. Back home, I smiled at the long orange rows of Chinese lanterns behind our house, waiting for harvest. The door of the storm cellar was still open from my trips to the canning room just hours before. Fall was here, all right, and now I felt a kinship with it. I opened the door of my spirit…and fall walked in, a welcome guest. Suddenly the day seemed pregnant with hope and possibilities.

> *"It is a common mistake not to leave the cares of the world from time to time to praise God and to rest in the peace of his divine presence for a few moments."*
>
> —BROTHER LAWRENCE

Oh, autumn is a hospitable season, opening doors to new and different choices. Your fall may offer chilly nights and warm evenings by the fireside with books you've saved till now. Popcorn sounds good again, hot cider is a must, and pumpkins decorate your doorstep. Autumn will bring you bright, bold mornings and a sense of repose as earth yawns before its winter rest. And you will sense the goodness inherent in repose: for the earth and for you.

On this autumn morn, you may decide to linger where once you rushed. See if you don't discover life works out just as well. You may decide to pray instead of worry, to rest in the unchanging promises of God instead of fretting.

So claim the gift of autumn and open it wide. It is for you! Savor the season, where once you rushed past it, and allow the multifaceted giftings of God to do their deep and soundless work in your soul.

I think I know why you made the seasons, Lord. At least I'll make a guess. I think it helps us to stop, look around, and take stock. It's that old thing about new beginnings. And you aren't bashful about the way you do it either. Wow! The colors of fall drip from your celestial paintbrush and wrap us in glory!

Lord of the seasons, in your divine wisdom you have chosen to move this earth through a parade of seasons, each beautiful, each unique, each standing importantly in its own particular regalia.

Autumn seems a kind of breathtaking parenthetical pause. It reminds me that all days are not the same—there is a gracious transition happening here, an annual resting of plants and flowers and gardens…and people. Fall reminds me to pause before the next season takes center stage, before all of nature tucks itself in bed for the winter.

Open my eyes, Lord! Open my heart! May I be in tune with the seasons and what you say through them.

"In you, I pray that what is scattered
in me may be brought together,
so that no part of me may be apart from you."

—SAINT AUGUSTINE

Listen to Winter

Whenever you choose to stop and rest, listen to the charms of winter. For you this season may be only a subtle shift from vibrant autumn to sleepy winter. Or it may be sharp and clear—a deep chasm between fall and spring. Winter may reveal itself only in dormant flowers, or it may send giant snowflakes drifting lazily from beneath the petticoats of the sky, falling like feathers soft shaken from some celestial pillow. In this vast and varied country, winter comes in different garments. Today, watch her approach, listening for her message.

Think of winter as the bringer of rest. Earth has been busy producing plants and food all season, and she is ready to move to the next season. So it is with your life. You have seasons of hard work and harvest, and then you are ready for rest. Is it not so?

"When we are continually on the go, giving away pieces of ourselves without taking time to replenish our spirits, we cannot feel bliss."

—ALEXANDRA STODDARD

Think back to summer when farmers laid seed in earth's plow-wrinkled bosom. With great thrusts of energy the land gave birth to plants. Day and night earth labored while you went about your business—while you slept and while you prayed and while you worked. And, in the fullness of time, the ground gave forth its bounty in a climactic and golden harvest. It was finished. The time for change had come.

The changing seasons speak to you—you who also labor but don't so easily rest. What good, after all, is a winter? Why is rest so necessary?

Think about the earth in its winter repose. A steady, quiet transformation occurs even as it lies still: Life-giving energy is being restored, recreated. Rest is birthing new life to come. For earth and for you, rest builds strength. Halting is but a part of working. Resting is but a necessary companion to industry. Winter, then, is an indispensable prelude to the season of rebirth.

Realization dawns, and your heart quickens at the truth of it: The quietude of winter, no matter where on earth you live, is a message from the God who created it. We are created with a need for rest. Quietness is the birth room of vigor.

Stop and listen well to the pronouncements of winter, and to the voice of a God who speaks clearly through a season.

God, you're talking again! And once again it's through a season. Winter is like a forced rest for the earth. You molded a whole globe that needs rest! And, I wonder, did you make me to need rest so I wouldn't get the idea that I'm invincible? That I'm an exception to the rules of nature?

Well, I'm hearing you today, Lord. What a crazed and arrogant pace I can get into—and what a price I pay! Maybe I should write into my day planner: REST—15 minutes. Hmm. That seems a little out of proportion, doesn't it? Most of my time is spent producing, and a tiny little chunk goes for rest. What kind of balance is that, really? Probably none at all. But at least it's a step. I think I'll pencil it in.

Lord, I'm glad you don't laugh at tiny, first steps and that you're there to catch me…because this is my baby step, and I'm liable to fall.

---

*"When women learn to care for themselves
because they are important in God's eyes,
they are much more apt
to avoid burnout and defeat."*

—SHARON HOFFMAN

You heavens above, rain down righteousness;
let the clouds shower it down.
Let the earth open wide,
let salvation spring up,
let righteousness grow with it;
I, the LORD, have created it.

ISAIAH 45:8

Start Anew in Spring

Spring! New beginnings! Fresh starts! Earth's initial trembling…
replete with seasonal longings for new growth and sunshine and
a sudden greening on the trees.

Whether or not spring dances through the doorway of winter or sashays softly into your area, you can still sense and often
smell the change in the air as winter wanes and the seasons
intersect with jubilance.

Listen! Hear the creeks burble more happily. Hear birds—
restless and giddy with nesting plans, singing stored-up songs
with a sky-blue energy. Sounds change in the spring, and if you
bend your ear to the newborn season, you hear the tones of
promise. There really are fresh starts! You really can begin again!
God's mercies really *are* new every morning—every new season!

"Each year when spring arrives, I feel almost giddy with relief that the winter is past. And I understand every cliché that was ever written about the season."

—MOLLY CULBERTSON

Stop now to notice the subtle changes in sun and clouds— in the fresh new leafings and the sprouting seeds and the brighter sky. The budding flowers seem to open within your own heart. The languid sun pours its private goblet of light and life without sparing, and plants press upward from brown earth wombs, pregnant with life and begging to be born.

Spring, for you, is a message of hope from the Creator: a bright banner spread maternally over the earth with your name on it. Today you will see spring with your eyes, and feel it with your heart, and take its message of hope deep into your soul.

God of all the earth…spring is so beautiful! I hardly know what to do with it…how to absorb it and take pictures with my heart so I can rewind them and view the loveliness again. You could have made an ugly earth or one that never changed. But you didn't, and I believe it was because you "so loved the world."

Lord, spring is so giddy—like a young colt loosed in a pasture. It's chock-full of youth and vigor, and there's a feeling of beginning again in the air. It's as if all the earth were starting over.

Can I start over again too? You know where I need to begin afresh without my telling you. And I know your glad answer before you give it. "Yes! A thousand times yes!" What a kind God you are, full of mercy and redemption. Here's my heart— take it and heal it and direct it on new paths for my good and yours.

I love the messages of spring. I feel a turning inside me toward happiness and joy and a fresh start. Maybe that's why you made spring... I don't know. But thank you from the bottom of my busy heart. Slow me down, even if it's against my will. Because I don't want to miss a single minute of this fresh season.

> *"There come days when the weather seems all whispering with peace, hours when the goodness and beauty of existence enfold us like a dry warm climate, or chime through us as if our inner ears were subtly ringing with the world's security."*
>
> —WILLIAM JAMES

Commit to the LORD whatever you do.

Proverbs 16:3

Take Pleasure in Daily Rituals

Everyone has daily routines and rituals. They are an integral part of life, and according to interior designer Alexandra Stoddard, they can take up as much as 95 percent of our time. Yet how often do we find ourselves reserving our enjoyment for the 5 percent of our time spent at "special" events?

Think with me: Our lives are made up of *every hour* of every day. Real life happens moment by moment, during all the daily time we spend in personal care, sleeping, eating, bathing, dressing, and so much more. And these very rituals can become part of the whole of a pleasing and rewarding life—if we will allow them to. For our hours do melt into days, and our days glide into weeks, and our weeks drift into years, and our years become a lifetime.

Look at the rituals of your own life: bathing, for instance. Do you shower quickly, just to get that task out of the way? Ah, then, let this interlude be your opportunity to make your shower a pleasant and satisfying ritual you look forward to and are reluctant to leave. How can you do this? Consider your before- and after-bathing clothes and your towels. Choose fabrics that soothe you by their texture and that stimulate you by their color and scent. Perhaps you'll decide to wear a silk garment on your way to the shower and snuggle into a clean, white terry robe after you're done. You might want to sprinkle a favorite talcum between bath towels or enhance them with a light after-shower spray. And then there is the heavenly delight of a warming rod for your towels.

> *"In the push and pull of contemporary living, we realize we have lost—maybe never possessed—a quietness of soul, a calm unassailed by the day's stresses."*
>
> —TIMOTHY JONES

As you prepare for your shower in your beautiful garment, you can smooth on a lemony or floral facial mask. As you step into the shower, try lathering yourself in a foamy, fragrant body wash before turning on the water, and then enjoy the exotic aroma as the hot water diffuses it. If you love bar soap, be sure to keep a special one on hand just for you—and use it for nothing and no one else.

As you wash your hair, do it with tenderness and consideration, using products you love to smell and love to feel as you lather. After you're rinsed, smooth silken lotion all over your skin. Take your time, and be loving to your body. Remember, the pleasure is in the doing, not in the finishing. Consciously choose to relish these quiet, private moments of your day that you may have thought were only in the way. Let them become part of the day's stream of joy.

Alexandra Stoddard speaks of rituals as "patterns you create in your everyday living that uplift the way you do ordinary things, so that a simple task rises to the level of something special, ceremonial, ritualistic." Your cleansing rituals can be boring or beautiful. You can merely brush your teeth, or you can *brush your teeth.* Find a beautiful glass to store your brush in and choose a favorite toothpaste that no one uses except you. Why not have a tiny "brushing center" complete with a candle! Listen to music while you brush. Look out the window instead of into the sink.

As you learn to take real pleasure in everyday events like these, you will be forming a necklace of momentary delights that become hours, which become days, which eventually translate into a life beautifully and happily lived.

Choose one of your current daily rituals to experience pleasurably. Think about what you could do to beautify and enhance it, to transform it into a small but grand occasion to anticipate—not something to "get out of the way" so you can get on with *real* life. For real life *does,* most surely, occur in the tiny moments, in the rituals of your every day.

God, I see something of your gentle heart in this idea. After all, you created me to have to do certain things to stay alive. I have to eat, and it takes so much time just to accomplish that! And then I have to get dressed, and make the bed, and do my hair, and file my nails, and on the list goes. If all this is merely "in my way," I'm wasting a lot of valuable time and missing a lot of enjoyment!

Since you made me to be a creature with needs, perhaps meeting the needs intentionally, with tenderness and even delight, is meant to be part of the abundant life you offer. I've been concentrating on the "big stuff," as though whatever that is constitutes real life. I never thought about all the precious moments I lose in hurrying to "get there" and to "get it done." I've slotted so much of my life into dutiful instead of beautiful, haven't I, Lord?

I think this interlude could be the beginning of something wonderful: the discovery of the small and the lovely…right under my feet. Lord God of the Universe! I'm amazed to realize that you stoop to fellowship with a woman who holds only a toothbrush in her hands.

> *"For a long time it had seemed to me that life was about to begin. Real life. But there was always some obstacle in the way…something to be got through first, some unfinished business; time to be served, a debt to be paid. Then life would begin. At last it dawned on me that these obstacles were my life."*

—B. HOWLAND

In quietness and trust is your strength.

ISAIAH 30:15

Pause for Tea

When morning drifts into afternoon, the body seems to call for a pause. Most days, you push away the urge, but today, do just the opposite. Today, accept the impulse to rest as a natural one, a needed one, and allow a short pause of refreshment. Walk into the busy middle of it all and command a time for yourself. And that time shall include tea.

Choose the finest dishes from your cupboard. And pick a single flower or select a single photo of someone you love to set on your tray, because doing so will announce to yourself that this is a personal, treasured time, not an ordinary one.

The cup you choose is beautiful; your teapot has special meaning. You choose a particular tea for the comfort of its fragrance as well as its taste: herbal and fruity, robust and fragrant. Or you choose something simple, like hot lemonade with a touch of lime juice.

Your teatime need not be hurried. You'll want to savor each sip and rest both your body and spirit. You may want to play instrumental music during your interlude. Or it may soothe you to read something inspirational. (No mail or newspapers allowed!) Resist answering your phone or being available to anyone for this little while. It's your set of moments to rebuild your strength and simply enjoy life.

> *"The little acts of kindness we do for ourselves express love…sipping a steaming cup of tea or soaking in a warm bath can replenish us so that we, in turn, can shower others with love."*
>
> —TERRY WILLITS

Nurse the cup as you cradle its warmth your hands. Enjoy the smooth contours and pleasing pattern, the gentle clink of cup on saucer. Savor the flavor of your drink and breathe in the fragrant steam.

You may want to purchase a packet of special teas just for times like this. Use them only for these special moments. They are small gifts to yourself, and you deserve them!

Depending on the time of day, you may want to "take your tea" in a soothing bath. Lean back on a cloth-covered bath pillow and surround yourself with an assortment of bubbling salts or silken oils.

The Spanish (and others) have their siesta. The English have their tea. These nations have the good sense to pause in the midst of grueling work or hot temperatures for a time of refreshment and revival. Perhaps it's time to begin a nurturing ritual of your own. Start with yourself…with teatime…today.

For some reason, Lord, I'm feeling a little embarrassed about even thinking of such a time for myself. But I guess it's worth a try—especially since you set the example of resting after you created this earth.

I know that taking special times for myself won't come easily or overnight. I feel too guilty too fast. But down deep, I know that I know that I know this is what I'm to do…what all of us can do because you give us permission. And so I'll pause for tea.

I'm so used to using the cracked cup and drinking on the go. To sit quietly and use the best cup I can find—perhaps even to have a "tea corner" just for myself—now that's a thought! I love it! No more paper or plastic for me! At least not all the time. Pretty cups nurture my soul and tell me it's all right to simply relax and enjoy. In fact, they tell me it's more than all right. It's a necessary nicety.

> *"Afternoon tea…the mere chink of cups and saucers turns the mind to happy repose."*
> —GEORGE GISSEN

Write down the revelation and make it plain on tablets.

HABAKKUK 2:2

Jot in a Journal

In *Care of the Soul,* Thomas Moore writes: "Soul thrives as we jot down a thought in our diary or note a dream and give body to a slight influx of eternity." My experience has proved Moore true time and again.

Jotting thoughts and noting dreams can become a holy act even when our scribbles are on the plainest of paper; a small spiral notebook will do. But if you want to make this interlude *really* special, you will need a very special kind of book to journal in…one that is beautiful and reflects who you are. When you handle it, you begin to gather a kind of nourishment from just touching a book of so fine a material, so colorful a cover, or so fragrant a page. The first touch is the beginning of your journaling experience. Hands like yours, so used to touching the everyday and the needful, will tremble with anticipation at touching this "holder of thoughts."

Your journal is a book written for your eyes alone. No other eyes need ever read what is recorded. It will be a place to bare your soul and reveal yourself to you and to your God. It will be a private forum of your unique concerns and brewing ideas and particular curiosities about life and living: a place to pour out your thoughts and observations and opinions and feelings without censor or judgment. You have to be able, when you journal, to shed your skin of "musts" and "shoulds" and be wholly and completely yourself.

Don't concern yourself with correctness of grammar or clarity of prose. The very act of journaling helps to refine your thoughts and sort through the jumble of feelings in your heart. You need never anticipate editing or pruning or rearranging of any kind. For if a journal is anything, it is a receiver of deeply personal hopes and dreams: the private book of *you*. This record of your journey will become a friend and confidant to help you along the way, an educator and guide as you look back over your journal in days to come.

The writing instrument you use when you journal can be ordinary—or as extraordinary as your one-of-a-kind journal itself. Consider writing with a fountain pen; it will require you to compose thoughtfully and with special care. Or choose a calligraphy pen with several nibs in an assortment of styles to inspire playfulness rather than carefulness. You may want to use several colors of ink in the same entry to express your moods as you write. See! A rainbow on paper! Red for excitement or passion. Yellow for happiness. Blue for sad feelings. Lavender to express contentment and tranquillity. Make your journal a work of art if you're so inclined. Draw or doodle in the margins. Write with crayons, felt pens, glitter pens! And keep these specially chosen items, together with your journal, in a place known only to you: perhaps tucked into a silken tote or a small cedar chest.

"It is a clear danger sign whenever any of us neglects the need for our own sacred space."

—ROGER MUHL

Your journal will be a place for the safe unraveling of your sometimes frayed edges and a repository of dreams not yet realized and ventures not quite dared. It will hold all your hopes and dreams with the tender reverence due such things. After all, mere thoughts and dreams often birth miracles.

And so, today, just for a while, dream and write and confide. Spread your soul on paper and shroud your dreams with prayer. And wait for them to be realized in God's time.

Lord, this small act, this interlude of time to myself, makes me feel rather like a queen. It also makes me feel a little selfish and uncomfortable. How long have I felt the urge to whisper and shout my feelings and dreams on paper? And how long have I set the whole idea aside, deeming it foolish or unproductive?

It's funny, Lord, but as I write in this journal, to no one in particular, I begin to see myself as I really am. I hear my thoughts better as they tumble out on a page, and I know that the truest essence of who I am is being opened to myself. You have known all along, haven't you? You've known the good as well as the bad, the ups as well as the downs. Why haven't you given up on me? I'm sure I would have! Yet you look in my heart day after day, reading all that's written there, and you accept, love, encourage, convict, redirect, and guide with infinite tenderness and wisdom. Thank you!

As I take this personal journey by journaling, unravel my heart and let me see what's in there. Let's look together. Keep writing on my soul, Lord. Edit as you will. When I look back on these words in days to come, I anticipate seeing the changes you've made…all just right for me because you love me.

---

*"Journaling helps clear your mind of clutter
and see patterns in your life more objectively.
It also lets you see God's faithful hand
unravel life's challenges."*

—Terry Willits

Let us acknowledge the LORD;
let us press on to acknowledge him.
As surely as the sun rises, he will appear;
he will come to us like the winter rains,
like the spring rains that water the earth.

HOSEA 6:3

Reflect on a Rainy Day

There's something about rain that brings a gladness to my soul. On a rainy day, I can't get caught up in all the outdoor chores waiting to be done: weeding the flowers, mowing the grass, pruning the bushes. A lot of people think rain is a depressing nuisance, but to me it's an invitation to be inside. Cozily so.

The invisible breath of God pushes plump rain droplets first westward, then eastward. Puffy dark clouds are edged in silver. Leaves drift lazily down, down, in a celestial ballet. On a rainy day the whole mood of nature is more serious, somehow. And that thoughtful tone beckons me to move into the interior of my soul as well as my house—to reflect and wonder and contemplate.

Your couch is a good companion for a rainy day interlude. Drape your favorite quilt or throw over your lap and plop down in front of a window where you can watch the stormy sky.

Open the window just enough to hear the keening wind chase its tail around the corners of your home and rustle off into the graying mists. Let the roaring of the heavens and the gleeful claps of thunderous celebration jolt you fully awake to the present moment. Hear fully the orchestral tunings and try to separate God's instruments from one another: the drum rolls in the distance, the insistent patter of raindrops against your sill, the irrepressible clashing of invisible cymbals, the steady thrum of the pounding downpour. Close your eyes and absorb the bold and fierce sounds of this symphony, composed somewhere in the castle yard of heaven and dropped over its parapets.

> *"We care for the soul by honoring its expectations, by giving it time and opportunity to reveal itself, and by living life in a way that fosters depth, interiority, and quality in which it flourishes."*
>
> —THOMAS MOORE

Notice the quiet seconds, the rests intertwined in the artfully composed storm. Soft sprinkles. Sudden bursts of sunshine, laid down like gold ribbons across the sodden sky. Enjoy these purposeful pauses in the masterpiece—intentional spaces in which you catch your breath and wait for more.

Then…a longer moment of silence. You wait and watch—suddenly there drops swiftly and soundlessly from the sky a jagged slash dancing brazenly across the satin sheen of black clouds. Lightning—followed by the lionine roar of thunder.

You continue to listen, noting the rhythm in the rain and its tempestuous turnings. It doesn't rain forever. The thunder isn't continual. The lightning comes and goes. Now loud as a lion. Now soft as a sleeping baby. Clouds darken, then brighten, then tumble and roll, then disappear.

You have stopped and you have listened well. In the rain, and in your own house, you have heard the voice of God and almost seen his face. You've heard his voice in the waters and seen him stride full-armored across the heavens, brandishing his flashing swords. You've seen his powerful play in the lively raindrops and claps of mighty thunder.

You wonder… Are storms divine wooings you only barely understand—regal reminders of the God who loves you? Your soul stands in respectful silence and then kneels before the Almighty who presents himself in a storm.

Lord of the raindrops…what can I say to you? How can I begin to tell you what it's like to see you yet not see you? Your power is in the storm. Your majesty is in a raindrop.

I am sorry I have merely endured so many times like this and only considered them a nuisance, an interference in my plans. God help me… I have become the victim of my own to do list. Today I welcome the rain as automatic permission *not* to do some things or go some places. It reduces my options. Yes! It's like heaven stooping down to give earth—and me—a much-needed drink.

God, forbid that I should let my life pass the way it has been passing. Teach me to revel in a raindrop! Clarify my vision about what's really important to your heart and what you want for me. Erase the tapes that keep spinning in my head about things that "must" be done—or at least record your sovereign will over them.

There is a way that seems right to a woman, but I think I often miss it. I veer off to the left and then to the right in search of accomplishment and acceptance, and I get lost! So you be my vision, Lord. Today let me see as you see and live as you would have me live.

"Will it not be employment enough
to accept gratefully all that is yielded me
between sun and sun?"

—HENRY DAVID THOREAU

When you are on your beds,
search your hearts and be silent.

PSALM 4:4

Stay in Bed for a While

Ever give yourself permission to sleep late? Ever think of shutting off the alarm and snoozing as long as your body needs it? Or does it seem impractical and self-indulgent to allow yourself such a luxury? Consider again Jesus' promise that if we come to him, we won't get another load of work, but (of all things) blessed rest. Surely a prolonged rest can't be as unspiritual as we might have thought.

So, think it over. Most of us need "catch up" days or, at the very least, lingering moments to regain our equilibrium. Resist and remain still. Renew and recharge. Revamp and recoup. Rest and restore.

Choose a morning to stretch out your time in bed. Make believe it's your private island: a hideaway all your own—a sumptuous feast of moments just for you. When you awake from your night's sleep, relish the fact that the next twenty minutes are yours alone. Don't answer the phone. Shut the door on your insistent urge to move directly into work and decide that, for now, your work is to rest.

"If you do not let your inner man waste away by neglect, then you will grow strong and vigorous inwardly. Spiritually, you will never die as you learn, by prayer and meditation, how to become liberated from all exterior pressures."

—SAINT AUGUSTINE

If you love to wake up to rich, hot coffee, you might want to plug in a coffeepot near the bed the night before and wake to its wonderful aroma. Pour yourself a cup in your favorite mug. Drink it slowly. Then cuddle down into the smooth sheets, fluff your pillows, and put on some relaxing music if it's near at hand. Or open a window and listen to the birds.

Believe it: You need not produce right now. You can't answer the door. You don't have to dress, or shower, or do your hair. Or anything. You don't need to plan (unless it refreshes you). All your concerns, all your challenges, all your to dos are in God's hands. Your only work right now is to put them there and leave them alone while he refurbishes your heart. Moments like these can be a monumental boost to your overall health and well being. Sleep if you need to. But, if not, dine on the wonder of just being awake and alive! Believe with all your heart that you are loved by God whether or not you can produce anything at all.

However you choose to relax, remember: It's your time to declare yourself unavailable to the world. Feast on the riches already in your life…and dream about the possibilities that lie ahead. Meditate. Listen for the voice of God. Expect. Celebrate.

Oh boy! Sleeping late? On purpose? I'm not used to this. In fact, I feel a tad ridiculous, kind of embarrassed and apologetic…to whom, I'm not sure. Frankly, this kind of thing is not something you admit to anyone. Imagine me telling ——— I stayed in bed this morning. It just wouldn't be acceptable. But then, most of the people I know seem to be running on empty.

I almost hate to admit it, but this feels wonderful… delicious. I suppose it wouldn't be so special if I did it every day, but I don't. So, guilt be gone! This little time of vacationing in bed is a candle in the dark…a beacon that guides me to part of the answer of to how to live a more rested life.

Jesus himself said: "It is written: 'Man does not live on bread alone, but on every word that comes from the mouth of God' " (Matthew 4:4). Lord, that's it! I've tried to live on "bread alone." I've been vandalized by the culture. I've been sweet-talked into insanity.

How is it that a little extra time in bed can make way for thoughts I never think? Oh, that's what this was all about? Thank you, Lord. I love the ways you get through to me!

> *"Though there are several areas in my home*
> *to which I like to steal away for a few moments*
> *with God, my bed is my favorite place*
> *for treasured quiet times. It is my sanctuary."*
>
> —TERRY WILLITS

I thank my God every time I remember you.

PHILIPPIANS 1:3

Appreciate Friends and Mentors

Today, why not spend some quiet moments simply thinking about the people who have made a difference in your life? Put on some soft music and light a fragrant candle. Curl up in a comfy chair in front of a fireplace or a favorite window. Sip herbal tea out of a pretty cup and let your thoughts wander a bit…float…go adrift. Get ready to think about friends and friendship, mentors and lessons learned. It's a wonderful way to count your blessings and to focus on people and memories that are lovely, admirable, and praiseworthy, as the apostle Paul urges all of us to do in Philippians 4:8.

Today, in these tranquil moments, recall the special people in your life who have had a way of dusting off your good intentions and helping you put feet to them. Remember the ones who have listened to your dreams and helped them to come true. Think fondly on the people who have simply loved you, just as you are. And those who have inspired you, comforted you, and made you laugh.

Settle deeply into your chair and remember the girl with the laugh who warmed you and sent you into spasms of laughter of your own; the teacher who noticed you and encouraged you to be your best; the neighbor who cared about you and showed it in practical ways; the women who have welcomed you into the inner sanctuaries of their hearts and made themselves at home in yours; the roommate who challenged your faith; the pastor who encouraged you at a low point; the friend who cried with you and helped you experience the balm of silence as well as the comfort of well-spoken words; the one who brought out mischief in you and called out your adventurous spirit; the one who inspired you to proclaim truth and create beauty; the one who smiled across a crowded meeting room or church sanctuary and made you feel less alone.

"Friendship is the marriage of the soul."

—VOLTAIRE

Good friends give us perspective when we need it most. Some rub against our rough edges and smooth us out. Some bring the blessed gift of laughter. Others listen so well, hearing the unspoken longings of our soul as well as our words. A few walk in uncanny tandem with us through years and years. Still other important people influence the course of our lives without ever even meeting us.

For me, books have been wonderful friends and mentors. They have given birth to many aspirations, encouraged my dreams, and developed my ideals and values. Books have befriended me and taught me and introduced me to a glittering array of people and ideas far from my personal surroundings.

In books I have met Eleanor Roosevelt and Thomas Edison and Martin Luther King and Michelangelo. Their dedication, their lofty thoughts, their contributions toward a better world have seeped inside me and changed the way I live. Those men and women I have never met personally planted seeds of good in my soul. Through books I have also gotten to know Harriet Tubman, C. S. Lewis, Corrie ten Boom, Mother Teresa, the multifaceted disciples of Jesus, and God himself. The power of books to introduce us to life-changing people and ideas is unlimited!

So, in these treasured moments, reflect on the goodness and wideness of God's love to you as you've experienced it through your particular friends and mentors—people God has sent especially into your life at just the right times to give you exactly what you need at the moment. And now trust and give thanks that he will continue to use people to bless and mold you all the days your life.

God, I count the human jewels with which you've adorned my life and realize I am wealthy beyond measure. People have shaped and formed me in so many ways—sometimes even in ways I haven't liked at the time. But now I see that you set those very people in my path—people who brought me both joy and pain. I thank you for both.

I joyfully thank you for the friends who have held lights to my path and made life easier to understand: friends, woven by your steady hand into the fabric of my life, each one giving me a glimpse of a different facet of your own nature. Jewels being polished for the Master's crown. Flawed, but moving in and out of my life with grace and courage.

Help me not to take these treasures for granted, Lord, or to believe I'm entitled to them. They are all gifts. May I never forget the good they have brought to my life. And help me discover ways to bless their lives in return. Mediate between me and my friends whenever necessary. Help me treat them as I want to be treated. Don't allow me to get too busy to be a friend, Lord! As Andy Stanley wrote, "Busyness destroys intimacy." Keep that foolish destruction from happening in my life.

Lord, as I meditate on the goodness of having friends and mentors, my thoughts turn to you—for you are the best friend and role model I could ever have. You know every single thing about me, yet you accept me and delight me and guide me continually on paths of peace. I puzzle over this amazing truth, yet I revel in it. Thank you for being my Friend for eternity.

"We have to know someone before we can truly love them. In order to know God, we must think about him often. And once we get to know him, we will think about him even more often, because where our treasure is, there also is our heart."

—BROTHER LAWRENCE

May the words of my mouth and the meditation of my heart
be pleasing in your sight, O LORD,
my Rock and my Redeemer.

PSALM 19:14

Ponder Great Poetry

Poetry has a way of opening new doors in our souls. In the words of a poem, our deepest yearnings are often brought out of hiding, as someone else says (in a most charming manner) what we ourselves long to say.

Poetry touches chords inside us and gives expression to our feelings. That's important because in the helter-skelter of our days, feelings often go unnoticed and unattended. Poetry attends to the soul in a unique way—like spending quality time with a true friend who knows our secret hearts.

If you already are a lover of poetry, you probably have favorite volumes on your bookshelf. Perhaps you haven't spent time with them for a while. Now is the time. For this handful of moments, scan the pages of an old friend until you find a poem or verse that is rich and meaningful to you. If you don't have old favorites, prepare for this interlude by checking out a few promising volumes from the library. Spend time with them until you discover the poets who speak your language.

"Vacations for the soul, pilgrimages of the spirit—that is what I have been exploring, and now make a part of my spiritual disciplines."

—TIMOTHY JONES

The Bible itself is lyrical and poetical—especially the psalms, which are actually songs recorded centuries ago. In those lyrics we find the entire spectrum of human emotion. And behind them, we meet very human men who were devoted to God—primarily King David. who wrote much of the book of Psalms. In his words—sometimes trusting and joyous, sometimes heavy with fear and lament—there is a continual flow upward from his heart to God's.

Now, consider carefully how you will set the stage for your reading: a place amenable and hospitable to the kind of concentration and engagement of mind and heart that poetry inspires. Perhaps you'll ponder best under an old tree, or beside a brook, or in a library, or in your favorite recliner at home. Choose carefully and well the place you read. Then allow this interlude to become an intimate visit with yourself, taking time to ponder the words that strike the chords of your inmost being. Which thoughts are "aha" thoughts? What feelings cry out to be visited? Spend time with them. Restless hearts often find repose and healing in a poem.

Rest, then, in a river of words carefully chosen and artistically arranged by a poet for someone, somewhere, someday: for you, during this tranquil interlude.

Dear Lord, thank you for giving me permission to address the part of me that calls out for attention. The very fact that this time feels a little strange to me will make it refreshing. I'm not sure what to expect, but this is a trip I'm taking, and I may as well stop at all the points of interest along the way. So here we go.

I have a funny feeling that something deep inside me is going to be touched in a way it hasn't been for a long time. And, for some reason, that's a little scary. I hide a lot of my feelings, you know. And poems…well, they call for a real engagement of the heart and soul. Some days I forget I even have a heart and soul! So I wonder what's in store for me today.

God, as I read, refresh me and refine me. Help me listen to my own heart as it is revealed to me. And help me simply lean into the poetry and revel in the words so pregnant with meaning. I imagine that if the king of Israel carved out time to write all the poems he wrote, I can find the time to read a few. I think I'll start right here in Psalms. Speak to me, Lord, through your Word.

"When I am restless, wanting something
to make me 'happy,' I know this is your call
to my soul. I'll feast on your Word,
and find my life in you."

—Saint Augustine

However many years a man may live,
let him enjoy them all.

ECCLESIASTES 11:8

Obey the Urge to Live *Now*

It was getting late. Evening pressed hard on the heels of day. Roy and I had just finished a leisurely dinner and cleared the table.

"Get the dishes done first and *then* take a walk," I told myself. When we built this home I had purposely said no to a dishwasher, believing this after-dinner time to be a revitalizing ritual—a time to think and plan and dream while I transitioned from day to night.

But as I began to wash the first dish, I was distracted by a low ribbon of sun lying across our row of sunflowers. I had feasted on this day already: so crisp and sunny. My morning glories had outdone themselves, spilling over the porch railing in heavenly blue abandon. Now I looked out from the kitchen window and could see our kitten chasing his elusive golden tail in a frenzied series of circular leaps and turns—a turbulent ballet of motion against the green grass.

Suddenly I realized there wasn't much time. I put the dishes to soak and obeyed the swelling of my soul. I donned a wide-brimmed hat and picked up a walking stick as I entered the forest of hardwoods just past our backyard.

> *"Believe it or not, it really is possible to slow life down and enjoy each moment. You really can have control over the sheer volume of activities and involvements that seem to drain your energy and motivation."*
>
> —THOMAS KINKADE

Wildwood, as we called that forest, fairly trembled with the Samson-like strength of late summer in its veins. It was crowned with the green glory of shining leaves and vast stretches of wildflowers. I simply could not resist the joy of such a walk. And so I walked. There was no question about the rightness of my forsaking the usual to bask in the incomparable present moment. To do otherwise, I felt, would be to forsake my Maker's calling on my soul. To live through the end of this day as if nothing at all had happened on earth would be to walk out on a symphony, to refuse happiness, to turn away a priceless gift.

The evening sun stole happily down into the heart of the woods, drenching the rich brown earth with molten gold. Leaves whispered and moved softly in the breeze, a private screen curtaining the antics of baby red squirrels. Two deer watched me, alert and graceful on their tiny spiked heels.

"Breathe deeply, woman," my soul seemed to whisper. "It is earth, and it is now. It may never again be exactly as it is this moment."

As I continued to walk, God hung the moon, a single pearl: gossamer against the dove-gray silk of the evening. A continual parade of color danced across the path beneath me: now pink, now gold, now scarlet—a palette of luminous hues moved about by God's celestial hand. I was transfixed, speechless.

As I emerged from Wildwood, the valley below me unfurled into undulating fields of corn, and tiny yellow lights blinked comfortably from farmhouse windows. Mallards flew low—slow-moving ink spots against a tangerine sky. Canada geese honked and soared, heading for the marsh. The farm families were gathering unto themselves for the night.

I walked on in silence up the steep, gravel drive toward home, reveling in the exquisite moonglow lighting my path. My spirit touched the hem of God's garments in gratitude—for my home, my family, my internal peace, my future with the Creator of all this beauty. A banquet of God had been spread like a feast before me, and from it I drew sustenance for my soul.

Such gifts are given every day…if we but obey the urge to open them *now*.

Dear Lord, don't let me miss too many sunsets, or sunrises, or anything else you've prepared for me. Break my legs if you have to, to keep me from running too fast past the perpetual feast you've prepared for the human beings you love so dearly.

As I think about it, all of this has been here waiting for me…every day and all along! These trees haven't moved in a hundred years! The birds are gliding over my head every day! And the sun… Oh, the sun! It introduces me to every morning with a smile and waves a comforting good-bye every night.

Where have I been? By leaning too far into my tomorrows, I have managed to miss many of the joys laid out in my todays. Cruel deception! "Now" is your gift to me, isn't it? Today is a ribbon of rainbows stretching from sky to sky, and now, finally, perhaps I'll begin to really see them.

"I come to my solitary woodland walk
as the homesick go home. I thus dispose
of the superfluous and see things
as they are, grand and beautiful."

—HENRY DAVID THOREAU

The voice of the LORD is over the waters.

PSALM 29:3

Swim at Daybreak

The sky spins mystical webs of black and gold at the dawning of day. Day is intertwined with night in a intricately woven fabric spanning the horizon, awakening the soul to mysteries yet unveiled by the God of the universe. At dawn, celestial curtains begin to lift, and morning spills with bright abandon over silvered water, catching moonbeams like fireflies. It is a time of beginning again—a promise of better things to come.

If you live somewhere or can visit a place where you have access to a natural body of water conducive to a morning swim, then you are indeed blessed! As the sun kisses trees and grass and flowers, the vast and varied rainbow of God's palette takes your breath away. Then, to glide soundlessly into the water at the break of day is to surrender completely to the ministrations of a loving Creator. To move with vigor and strength in a lake, a pond, a pool, or an ocean is to prepare the body and soul for whatever follows. To splash and dive and float and laugh into the sunrise is a gift to the self.

So, child of God, glide through the liquid satin or impetuous waves: through them and on top of them. Dance with joy through the water because God created the water and surely enjoys your enjoyment of it.

} *"Think big thoughts but relish small pleasures."*

—H. JACKSON BROWN JR.

And after a playful swim, wrap up in a thick, cozy towel and sit quietly at the water's edge, simply observing the clouds in their passionate waking undulations. It is a time to release your concerns to almighty God, to regather yourself, and to breathe deeply of the pristine air. And, finally, to rise to meet the day.

_____

Lord! I can hardly speak for the glory of this morning: the beauty around me, the freedom and the opportunity to simply enjoy what you've made, and the very real sense of your presence. How is it that you seem to speak so powerfully in and through the quietest times? How is it that you say so much without saying a word? I hear a sermon in the breeze and a wise teaching in the waves.

I know very little for certain, but I know that you are here and that you are God. The friendship between us is invisible yet tangible—like silken threads of a cobweb: now glistening, now gone…but still there.

Speak to me this new day, Lord, of your love. Speak to me softly, like a mother. Speak continually and speak in ways I can hear. This is my request…and this is your pleasure.

Ah, again I say I know very little for certain. But I know you are here. And now, as always, it is enough.

"The most beautiful castle filled
with the richest foods and finest music could
never come close to satisfying our primary
need for a relationship with God."

—TERRY WILLITS

Wash me, and I will be whiter than snow.

PSALM 51:7

Soak in a Bubble Bath

People rarely take baths any more. Long, leisurely soaks of thirty minutes or more seem to have no place in most women's lives. But you, during this interlude, are going against the tide. You are choosing the pure pleasure of the bath! A bath, thoroughly experienced, will soothe you and carry you, for a time at least, into a pampered sanctuary of solitude. It's definitely half an hour well spent.

Prepare, first of all, by turning on some favorite music. Choose music you love, music that weaves a spell of soothing relaxation. It will be a pillow for your body and spirit. Ideally, your music will be wordless, calling for no engagement of your mind, no response, no reaction. It will be merely a backdrop for your thoughts, curtaining off your daily responsibilities. Oh joy!

You will want to lock the door if possible, and put a sign on the outside that says, "Back in half an hour."

Light some candles and place them in front of your bathroom mirror to double the loveliness. Prepare your bath as you would a delicious dish for the table: with care and thought. As you fill the tub with warm water, scent or soften it. Add bubbles, lots of bubbles! Bring luxurious grooming aids within reach. You might choose foamy cleansers or facial masques, special aromatic soaps saved just for this time, colorful bath beads filled with silken oils, soft washcloths or nubby sponges. Add whatever will make this a luxurious time—one set apart just for you.

"Honor yourself today with a time of sheer comfort."

—SHARON HOFFMAN

When everything is ready, slide down into your bed of water and rest your head on a bath pillow or a rolled-up towel. Close your eyes or watch the candles flicker. Breathe deeply and often until at last you have truly "come away." Then, for a time, do nothing at all except receive the comfort of the water. Let it allay any discomfort of body or heart.

If your candles are scented, you will have begun to enjoy the fragrance by now and find yourself called deeper into reverie. Focus on the candle flames and simply enjoy. You may find yourself wanting to utter a simple prayer. One word. Two. A sentence. Openings of the soul. Connectings to God. Then, once more, eloquent silence.

The ritual of the bath should proceed slowly and with purpose. Drizzle the water down your arms. Smooth the soap onto your skin. Inhale the luscious fragrances. You're tired of rushing. So float your tired limbs. Give yourself to the gentle water.

This small getaway can gather together all your scattered parts. You will find yourself lifting them quietly and simply into the hands of a God who gladly partners with your concerns. Your soul is quieted. Your heart is nourished. You are made whole once again.

Follow your bath with a warmed towel, a sprinkling of talcum, a spritz of cologne, a smoothing of the richest creams. It is a womanly ritual of utmost value: a vacation in a tub.

This is glorious, Lord. And so easy, so doable. I think thirty minutes in this lovely bath will do almost as much for me right now as a day away from duties and responsibilities. It's like a bouquet of flowers fresh from the garden. It's like stepping on shore and finding it heaven. I feel twenty pounds lighter, and even that is a treat in itself!

I love this half darkness…the candlelight and the shadows dancing across the ceiling. I love the sense of being far away on some remote island. And I love the heady fragrances.

But you know all that, don't you? Simple pleasures—like a walk in the garden with the first human being you created— were your idea in the very beginning. Whoever thought up rushed morning showers anyway? I'm sure they weren't your idea! No wonder our grandmothers looked forward to their long, Saturday-night soak in the tub beside the roaring wood stove.

You know, Lord, this is just one of the small ways I plan to start recapturing my lost moments and the simple joys all

around me. And I'm hearing that my plan is all right with you.
After all, a bath does so much more than simply remove dirt.

---

*"In his presence nothing really matters…nothing is
of importance except attending to him.
We allow inner distractions and frustrations
to melt away before him as snow before the sun."*

—RICHARD FOSTER

*Dear children, let us not love with words or tongue
but with actions and in truth.*

1 JOHN 3:18

Write a Letter of Love

So few of us write letters anymore. We have e-mail now. Voice mail and faxes. Modern technology has given us the opportunity to nurture a relationship with someone without ever even meeting that person or even hearing her voice. And there are some good things about this. But a handwritten letter… Whose heart doesn't leap at an envelope in the mailbox addressed personally to her? When was the last time you received a letter of love? Or wrote one?

I don't have time to write letters, you might think. *I can't even keep up with my e-mails or return my phone messages.* But think about it for a moment. It takes only thirty minutes (or less!) to sit down with pen and paper and send a message of love to someone who will be thrilled to receive it. This interlude—writing to a loved one—will nurture your own heart and bless another's in ways you might not even imagine.

So let this be your time to write…to do so slowly and thoughtfully, with care and a loving heart. There will be a difference between this epistle and an e-mail message composed on the spot and often carelessly arranged. This will be wholly unique and highly valued by the recipient, for letters of substance have become rare. Write as if you are sculpting: with a vision of the one you are writing and a passion to create a gift worth savoring and keeping.

Choose a place in which to write that soothes and nurtures you—a bench beside a lake, a picnic table in the park, a special writing desk, a quiet corner in your favorite coffee shop, even while soaking in the tub! Wherever you choose, make sure there is a measure of solitude and beauty, for writing produced in such a place conveys a sense of peace to the one you write to.

So to whom will you write a letter of love today? It need not be someone far away; it could be your husband or child or best friend. Or you might settle on a person who needs love in a particular way right now. Focus your thoughts on that person for a few moments before you begin and walk in his or her world. What is he feeling? What are her needs? Before you begin to write, breathe a prayer for this person you want to love with words.

Now, choose a pen—not just any pen, but one that slows you down and expresses your personality on paper. Watch your own flair emerge as you dot and flourish and swirl pen against paper. Turn the nib of a fountain pen this way and that, and create a letter lovely to look at and easy to savor. A wide nib will give you graceful, flowing letters. A colorful felt-tip pen will create a mood and help you write with gentle ease. You might want to choose several colors of ink in order to add meaning, fun, and vigor to your letter. Try writing the whole letter at an angle across the page, beginning at a corner. Or write in a circle, from the center to the edges of the page. Why not? Think what fun it would be to receive such a personally designed, creative masterpiece!

> *"The art of art, the glory of expression and the sunshine of the light of letters is simplicity."*
>
> —WALT WHITMAN

Whatever you do, be sure to write with a purpose: to express love and to bless someone's heart. And, in the process, to bless your own as well.

When you're finished, tuck inside the envelope a tea bag or some tiny paper hearts or bits of glittery confetti. Spray a favorite perfume on the page, or dab a bit of scented oil on a cotton swab and fragrance the inside of the envelope. Tuck in a photo that will bring a smile or a stick of gum for a child.

This letter that has taken so little time to write—your personal messenger of love—will have the stamp of your soul on it. It will bond you to someone you love in a singular way, because letters, penned in a tranquil hour, convey a heart's truest sentiments.

God, I'm thinking about the letter you wrote to me...to all of us. You took such a long time to write it—to decide what you wanted us to know and what you didn't. You used so many words to reassure us of your love. You didn't hold back at all in lavishing your love as you wrote your heart to humanity through hand-picked scribes centuries ago.

O Lord, I love your letter, the Bible! It teaches me, it informs me, it reveals your deepest essence. It gives me guidelines for abundant living. It shines a beacon on my sin and then covers my confession with forgiveness and love. It tells me of One who so loved me and all of us that he gave... and gave...and keeps on giving. I love that your letter has been preserved for me throughout the ages and that I can wrap my life in its truths.

Your letter...to me...written in red.

"I have a friend who lives one block away and we share hand-delivered notes. There is a special magical quality to these hand-delivered notes because they arrive at odd, unexpected times, at isolated moments when the regular mail doesn't come—early morning or Sunday afternoon."

—ALEXANDRA STODDARD

Faithfulness springs forth from the earth,
and righteousness looks down from the heaven.
The LORD will indeed give what is good,
and our land will yield its harvest.

PSALM 85:11-12

Take a Stroll of Wonder

Have you seen anyone strolling lately? Better yet, how long has it been since you strolled? Probably not since powerwalking caught the national fancy. You can tell a powerwalker by the pained expression on his or her face. Now if it's true that power-walking causes pain, I for one opt for pleasure. I choose to stroll! Care to come along?

If you decide to stroll today, don't cover your ears with earphones or every inch of your body with clothing. A stroll is an occasion to free the whole person, not hamper or hinder or bind. It's a time to let the wind mess up your hair and carry away your thoughts and enlarge your heart toward God.

So come along. Let your stroll be slow, leisurely, explora-tory. Along the way, stop…and consider what you see. Admire it. Touch it. Smell it. Think about it. Ask why and what and where and when. Really listen to the birds and the wind and see the cows and cars and children and dogs. Practice thinking: Become your own commentator on world events, exercising the power of individual thought.

On your stroll, choose not to look only straight ahead because getting it over with is not your goal: Enjoyment is. Be open to diversion and unexpected delights and sunny surprises. Wander down an unfamiliar path, perhaps with a walking stick, just because there's a bit of adventure in the unexplored. Stop and pick some sun-ripened berries or stoop to gather summer wildflowers or autumn leaves.

"In my experience, people with a simple faith and a simple, childlike outlook seem to be more open to kairos [God-controlled] moments. They are not so busy doing and achieving and creating their own self-constructed destiny that they miss the hidden treasures that are waiting in the ordinary events of life."

—CLAIRE CLONINGER

Take the time to wonder about those who strolled here before you...and invent lives for them and their children. At this juncture, you will almost feel as if you've touched another generation, and you may wonder why God put you here, now, instead of somewhere else at a whole different time. What does he have in mind for you? These are all thoughts of wonder, and there's only a baby step between a thought and a prayer.

So, then, take a stroll and begin to wonder. Take time to reflect and imagine and appreciate. Strolling will be a surprise gift to yourself, a delight to your heart. Stroll…not to accomplish, but to relinquish. Stroll to receive the gifts of God into your heart. You can commune with God wherever you are, you know. Communion is not restricted to a ceremony within church walls, but reaches out to us in everyday places and ordinary moments.

God, it feels so good to simply stroll! I'm so tired of making every second count according to society's standards. Strolling may not be popular, but it feeds my soul. Who cares if I have a great body, whipped into shape by relentless exercise, if my heart and soul are sick and tired? Who really cares if my heart beats so many times a minute if I have squeezed the very life out of life by punching in too many "oughts" and "musts"? Whose idea was it to manipulate and manage every minute of my life in such a way that I'm left with no time to take a stroll of wonder?

Well, I intend to stroll a lot more. Strolling is soul work! It's a tool in your hand, Lord. On a stroll, I'm open to sassy surprises and pungent smells and new sights: And I am free to think and ponder and pray and simply enjoy this world you've put me in for these moments in time.

Thriving! That's what strolling is about, isn't it, Lord? Not merely surviving, but thriving. Yes! And you are around every

corner and under every rock and in the whisper of the wind.
And I want you. So I'm all for strolling, world, ready or not!

> *"Sometimes when you are working*
> *within me, bringing my scattered self*
> *to you, you draw me into a state*
> *of feeling that is unlike anything*
> *I am used to, a kind of sweet delight."*

—SAINT AUGUSTINE

Listen to the Songs
of the Night

There's something about evening, after the sun says good-bye to the day, that opens a new room for the soul to enter and explore. In a darkened room—especially in a cold winter with a fire crackling in the fireplace—or under a night sky, all pretense falls away. It doesn't matter if our hair looks good, or if our clothes are pressed, or if we forgot to brush our teeth. No one can see. Besides, the darkness becomes stronger than any of these concerns—a gentle robing for our true selves.

In the kindness of the dark, we need not focus on our flaws, our extra weight, our aging, our failures. Instead, there is a sense in which our most authentic selves come out in the darkness. Some say that who we are in the dark is who we really are.

How very good, then, that the God of light, who pierces

the darkness and sees our truest selves, will not be shocked! For by his own confession, he loves us without condition, with an everlasting love that transcends all earthly days and nights. In the dark, we come to him without shame or sham. Truly and openly we come. Even if we don't officially pray, he hears our hearts.

In the heart of darkness, somehow, our souls are set free. It is a place of release. Pent-up tears of joy or pain can flow: raw and real. We have no expectations to meet. Breathing comes more easily—deeper. Dreams surface—longings show themselves. And buried wishes come out to play. All these, and more, are the stuff we're made of and the stuff that seems to surface when we slow down for a little while.

> *"There are times when my spirit escapes the world completely and soars above the earth's atmosphere to where unlimited freedom exists."*
>
> —JOYCE HIFLER

So tonight choose to do just that. Turn on some soft, dreamy music or opt for no music at all. Light a fire in the fireplace or a candle on the window sill. Or open the curtains and let the moon be your shadowmaker as it waltzes into the room with its Mona Lisa smile. It's a whole new world in the shadows.

Or step out into the yard and listen to the crickets or tree frogs or owls or coyotes. The creatures of the night. Watch the lightning bugs as they scatter a blanket of diamonds in the air. Listen for the sounds of children or animals as they, too, prepare for the night. Listen to the songs of the night and be enchanted.

In a matter of minutes, your spirit will be calmed and your head cleared. You will begin to hear the voice of God. God created the day, and in it we work, we labor, we strain, we create, and we exert ourselves. God also made the night and we rest— we are recreated; we prepare for yet another day. In moments of resting in gentle darkness, we come home to ourselves and to God, to a place of quietness and joy. We make the night our own. And we dine on its pleasures.

Dearest Lord, I feel kind of funny doing this. I mean, this isn't exactly something one writes into her Day-Timer. Oh, well. I've asked you to show me how to rest and how to hear your voice, and so I'm going for it. But this is only a test! Action I know. And work I know. But this? This I do not know.

So hello, God. Here I am. Simply sitting still in the dark. I'll bet you never thought you'd find me here, did you? Frankly, neither did I. Lord, are you looking in my heart right now? Do you see what's there? Is it okay with you? Do you see the tears? Do you see all the questions I've been grappling with? Can you see my fear of what's ahead? Do you see my secret wishes and joyful dreams? I'm glad that the light of your love makes me safe here, right where I am tonight.

Funny how I hear so much more when I listen in the dark. I can hear the smallest noises, the sound of my own beating heart, the whisper of your Spirit. My mind has slowed down and my breathing is easier. The darkness is like a velvet cloak, sumptuous and satisfying.

Renew me tonight, Lord. Hear the whispers of my heart…and shepherd me through the days to come. I've been told you are always present—even in the shadows. And now I know it's true.

"As we open our hearts to embrace God's Sabbath opportunities, we will be discovering this delightful and freeing reality—that earth's apron is covered with little pockets of heaven's rest for those who will stop to find them."

—CLAIRE CLONINGER

From the fullness of his grace we have all received
one blessing after another.

JOHN 1:16

Treasure
the Grace Notes

"Grace notes," explains the dictionary, "are musical embellishments—notes not necessary to the melody." In our lives, grace notes are the unexpected joys, the unplanned blessings, and the surprise packages that expand our enjoyment of the "music."

No life is completely without grace notes. On any given day, we are all, no matter what our circumstances, blessed with moments inserted by God to draw us to praise him and to expand our thoughts beyond our troubles, to lift up our eyes beyond and past the sordid and the mundane and to focus on him. Grace notes are the messengers of God to remind us of the reality that all truly is well with our souls, regardless of our feelings or circumstances.

Step outside, then, with your eyes as well as your feet. Fix your eyes on a grace note. Observe your home, your yard, your view. Think of yourself as a planting of God in this very spot. Whatever is good, whatever is lovely, think long and hard on these things, because the God of peace will be with you in increasing measure as you do (see Philippians 4:8-9).

Think about your own body for a moment. Does your mind immediately go to the member that's aching or out of sync? Why not remember that most of your body is well. And why not realize that the ailing part is usually in the process of being healed. While you're at it, let your mind embrace the mind-boggling truth that in eternity, your entire mind, body, and soul will be perfectly well and that life on this earth is so very brief. Meanwhile, choose to praise God both for the health in those parts of you that are well and for the myriad ways your body still serves you and can serve others.

When thinking about the grace notes in your life, let your heart guide you to those you love. You may want to leaf through a photo album, focusing on the faces of special people and good times. There is unexplainable joy and power in memories of love and rich fellowship. As you reflect on each loved one who comes to mind, ask God to strengthen their strengths and minimize their weaknesses. As you move through this exercise, you may find yourself wanting to communicate with some of these people. By all means, do so! A quick e-mail note will do, but a handwritten note in the mail means more. A simple sentence is all it takes to express your gratitude for the grace this person has brought into your life: "I am thinking about you today and thanking God for how he's touched my life through you." Or "I'm missing you today and praying that God will send you grace notes, just as he sent them to me through you." Or "Remember when we…?" a question that can flood a loved one's heart with a warm memory. A short, heartfelt note of grace and gratitude will nurture a special relationship.

Now think about yourself and your life right now. Do you have any opportunities that you didn't have before now? Are there things you can do now that you couldn't do earlier? Name the opportunities God has strewn generously across your path. Can you think? Can you plan? Can you organize? Can you nurture? Create? See? Visit? Travel? Invent? Write? Cook? Deliver? Call? Pray? Your list of opportunities may actually be very, very long. Surely your life is multifaceted and full of a thousand doors you can open. When viewed through this lens, even the smallest opportunities become occasions to praise the God who gives them to you.

> *"People who celebrate spontaneously and without affectation do it because they know there is always something to celebrate."*
>
> —VICTORIA MORAN

Can you listen to or create music? Then, even if you can do nothing else, your soul can still take flight! To be able to listen to or play or create music is a gift to be unwrapped every day and enjoyed with delight and thanksgiving. Take a moment now to put on your favorite music. Close your eyes and lean back and listen to every note, every nuance. Try this after dark, on a snowy night, with a fire in the fireplace. It will take the chill off the coldest of days and stoke the fires of your heart.

Is there provision for your basic needs in life? It is a grace note. Is there more than one garment in your closet? It is a grace note. Is there a roof to protect you from storms? It is a grace note. Is there love in your life? It is the sweetest grace note of all. Pause now to lift a prayer of thanks and find yourself worshiping the God who will provide, Jehovah-Jireh.

Worship is also a grace note. We come to God, palms upraised, with nothing much to offer except our imperfect love and our bottomless need. Our hearts yearn for him, and we find ourselves lost in wonder, love, and praise. We are fully with God when we worship him, whether in private or in public. Problems shrink. Sorrows are soothed. Joy expands and overflows. Oh, worship is definitely a grace note! We come to give, and we are changed by his giving.

Think about the love of God. Believe it. Receive it. Open your heart in gratitude as you reach out to embrace his abundant grace. His grace notes are everywhere. They flow in an endless river, shimmering with divine love. Almighty God! Thank you for lace-edging our ragged worlds with your bountiful grace!

---

erciful God, I have taken so much for granted! And I keep wanting more! I'm just plain appalled at my callous

disregard for your generous provision and your multiple blessings. I walk past grace notes every day yet have the nerve to ask
for "more" and "better"!

Lord, I haven't stopped to take a good look around me
for a long time. But I'm here now. My ears are open and I'm
listening. The eyes of my heart are ready to see. And I do!

I want to say thank you from the bottom of my heart for
the ways you care for me. Just stopping to notice all you've
given me relaxes me. Suddenly I remember that happiness
and security aren't out there somewhere, but instead, they're
all around me because they're found in you. Yes! Happiness
and security are right here…now.

Lord, I look in my closet, my garage, even my kitchen,
and see more than enough. I think about the ways I have
loved and been loved: more than enough. My heart is filled
to overflowing with the bounty you provide.

From you, Lord, I have received one blessing after another,
and I treasure each and every grace note in my life today.
Forgive me for the shortsightedness and ingratitude that often
cloud my vision. You are a generous God! "Surely goodness
and love will follow me all the days of my life, and I will dwell
in the house of the LORD forever" (Psalm 23:6).

"All shall be well and all shall be well
and all manner of thing shall be well."

—JULIAN OF NORWICH

Perfume and incense bring joy to the heart.

Proverbs 27:9

Indulge in a Fragrance

Time flies when we women are shopping! Yet why not insert a tiny time just for yourself into your next duty-full shopping trip? It could turn an ordinary, completely forgettable errand day into a delicious memory.

On this day go in search of fragrance. Consciously indulge the gift of olfactory perception God has given you. Think… When was the last time you even considered the simple delight that can be drawn in through your nose, the bouquet of delicious treats that are readily available in this fascinating world of ours? As Alexandra Stoddard writes, "All of us are orbiting like stars in the universe. We can't have our dance card filled for the rest of our lives, because we need spaces to allow for serendipity." And what simpler serendipity than a whiff of a pleasant aroma?

So today make space for sensual delight by choosing to visit a store that carries an extensive line of fragrances: perfumes and lotions and soaps and room sprays and candles and incense and all things created to give a woman pleasure. Seek out a variety of scents, from spicy or exotic, to floral or fruity, to piney or musky. Simply indulge in whatever gives you olfactory pleasure. And let your mind wander as you do. Notice which fragrances bring back sweet memories. Which ones get your heart beating faster…or slower? Close your eyes and inhale, considering the words of an anonymous someone who knew that "a fragrance dresses a dream."

> *"It doesn't so much matter what you do, as long as you smile when you remember it."*
>
> —VICTORIA MORAN

As you indulge yourself—inhaling delicious scents, rubbing yummy creams into your skin, trying different perfumes on your wrist—notice which product you're drawn to like a magnet. And, if you can, buy it to take home with you so you can continue this personal indulgence again tomorrow and the day after! Be sure whatever fragrance you choose suits you and the life you live. The fragrance a woman wears reflects, to some degree, who she is and what she does. When others catch a whiff of this particular fragrance, it should remind them of you. Of course, if you can have different fragrances for different occasions, that's wonderful! But each should, in its own way, say "you."

You might consider getting a fragrance to save for special occasions only: an anniversary, or Sunday, or Friday nights, or bedtime, or after a luxurious bath. This is a subtle and delightful way to celebrate the moments God gives you for personal refreshment and joy, to set them apart as special.

Most surely the God who filled the whole earth with an abundance of fragrance smiles gently upon us when we indulge in moments of pure personal delight. As you allow yourself time for simple joys like this, you may not be able to articulate what they really mean to you. Perhaps you will only be able to say, with the poet Edna St. Vincent Millay, "I only know there came to me a sense of glad awakening."

Hmmm… This is really something, Lord. You are a God who not only creates vast and inconceivable beauty, but who offers it to me over a counter in a stoppered flask or plastic bottle!

You, who walk with me through everyday routines as well as the rocky and brushy terrain of life, also enjoy my enjoyment of what you've made! You spoke and it was formed. You breathed and there was life. You lifted your scepter and clothed the earth in sumptuous, undreamed-of beauties. And you did it all with us in mind.

You could have made everything on earth without fragrance, but you didn't. This must mean that scent is a part of the sensual pleasure you planned for us from the beginning. The breeze blows, and it's fragrant. A leaf drifts down, and it carries with it a lingering aroma. I bury my nose in a flower and am overcome with the perfume.

Thank you for the gift of fragrance, Lord, and for the simple joy it ushers into otherwise mundane moments.

"We are constantly gifted with a stream of 'little things' which can help restore our mental and emotional balance and provide us with a rich resource for happiness— if we learn to appreciate them."

—DR. ARCHIBALD HART

He leads me beside quiet waters,
he restores my soul.

PSALM 23:2-3

Sit Beside the Water

When we long for rest and peace, many of us seek out water. Water soothes, softens, and even washes away concerns. It can redress worries in such a way that we can't even recognize them.

To sit beside a body of water, arms around knees and ears open to its liquid undulations, is in itself enough to revive and rejuvenate almost any woman. A bubbling brook, a placid pond, a rushing river, an enormous ocean—all are wonder-filled places for listening and rest. The longer we are still, the more we see happening in the underwater world of God's creation. Fish splash. Frogs croak. Water bugs jump. Otters frolic. Nature seems active and playful. Perhaps the water and its inhabitants have something important to say to our scattered souls.

Decide today to take your interlude by the water. Simply watch it. And if you find a place where you can wade or dangle barefoot toes, all the better. For a little while you will become a child again; you will let your soul come out to play.

"In the solitude afforded to me at the sea edge I constantly discover a dimension of divine serenity that is a balm to my spirit, a deep therapy to my soul."

—PHILLIP KELLER

Allow whimsical and comical and even silly thoughts to come to mind. They are brooms, sweeping away adult mental clutter. Imagination will set your heart free to wander. Let it take flight, open to receiving the joys of nature created for you by a loving heavenly Father.

You might consider having a private picnic beside a brook or a lake. I love a place where the grass is "mowed" by the cows pastured there and where tall trees offer shade. Find a place where a stream sallies through the woods, and the water is clean and pure. Grab a beach chair and plant yourself on the shore. Choose a place that reminds you of the Garden of Eden, God's grand and gracious beginning. And think happy thoughts.

In the absence of other people, you will sense more vividly the invisible presence of the living God. After a time, when your soul has bent its ear to the earth and felt the pulse of God in the waters, you will feel cleansed and refreshed and ready to return to whatever else the day holds for you. An energy will have been imputed to you simply because you showed up. You will be reluctant to say good-bye, but glad to tuck this sweet interlude into a secret vault in your heart where you can revisit it whenever you need to "come away."

Dear God, how you speak through nature! I hear you so well through the crashing of the waves and the gurgling of the brook and the splashing of fish and frogs. You are everywhere I turn! I treasure these moments when you reveal yourself to me. I need only take the time to stop, look, and listen.

I'm looking forward to the day when I see you in all your glory—face to face. There's so much I want to know like…how did you decide what color to paint the sky? And why is the ocean so big? And how did you make your whole creation so beautiful and yet so magnificently functional?

Thank you, Lord, for this interlude in my busy life. Thank you that you've given me streams of rest to enter into, rivers of your love to swim and play in to my heart's content. I'm so glad I took the time today to just sit beside the water.

> *"Each of us lives quite differently, and we have our own unique patterns, rituals, and schedules. But I've come to realize we all share the need to get away from everything and everybody and to be alone— regularly."*
>
> —ALEXANDRA STODDARD

By wisdom a house is built,
and through understanding it is established;
through knowledge its rooms are filled
with rare and beautiful treasures.

PROVERBS 24:3-4

Embrace Your "Home" Work

What do you think of the work you do in and around your home? Is it something that just gets in the way of real life? Or are the tasks of cleaning and cooking and mending and washing at least partially a pleasure?

For many years, I believed I was doing "all that work" for my family. It slowly dawned on me, however, that I was doing it as much for myself as for them, and even more important, I was doing it for God. He was my overseer, no matter what work I did.

Think with me for a few moments… When machines began to reduce some of our physical chores (sometime in the 1930s), we were "freed" to do other (better?) work. But by the 1970s women were becoming vocal about the emptiness in their lives. Betty Frieden offered her solution in *The Feminine*

Mystique, and women began to enter the workforce in droves. Of course, working outside their homes was in addition to continuing to work at home. What first seemed like a new freedom became for more and more women an impossible task. A woman's work was, in fact, never done! Women in the 1980s were vocal about their stress, and by the mid-1990s the pendulum was swinging: More women were choosing to work at home and from home.

Even in our homes, our endless activity threatens to drown out the voice of God, who all along has simply called you and me to a balanced, reasonably occupied life. For a few moments, put aside your to do list and *all* your assumptions about what you "should" do and "have to" do today. When you're over-busy, it's hard to imagine how life *might* look instead of how it *does* look. So choose to come away for a while and consider the pleasures and satisfactions of your "home" work. And then choose for yourself a task that gives you true satisfaction.

"Your home should be a greenhouse where you flourish to your full potential."

—VICKI KRAFT

Do you love gardening? Then dig your hands deep and with love into the earth God created. Listen to his messages to you that come through the very plants and seeds and flowers you tend.

Or consider my friends who hang their laundry outside for the pure pleasure of it…for the fresh smell, for the joys of being outdoors, and for seeing the clothes and sheets and towels billow in the breeze. These women have not given up all their satisfactions to "timesaving" machines.

What will it be for you? Could ironing be a time to relax your heart and mind, to meditate and pray and daydream? Could you find simple joy in washing dishes today?

I have intentionally chosen not to have a dishwasher because, for me, dish time is a tranquil interlude slipped in-between day and night, where I am alone with my thoughts. With love, I touch the glass and see it sparkle. With satisfaction, I scrub the black off the pan and see it shine. Because of me, it shines.

Is there some work you've given over to a machine that may give you simple joy if you take it back into your own hands today?

In my laundry room hangs a journal page from a woman of yesteryear. It reminds me of the simple and sometimes sublime work awaiting me at home. Here is a great-grandma's account of her washday:

1. Bild a fire in back yard to heet kettle of rain water.
2. Set tubs so smoke won't blow in eyes if wind is pert.
3. Shave one hole cake, lie soap in bilin water.
4. Sort things, make three piles. 1 pile white. 1 pile cullord. 1 pile work britches and rags.

5. Stur flour in cold water to smooth, then thin down with bilin water.

6. Rub dirty spots on board, scrub hard, then bile, rub cullord, but don't bile—just rench and starch.

7. Take white things out of kettle with broom handle, then rench, blew, and starch.

8. Spred tee towels on grass.

9. Hang old rags on fence.

10. Pore rench water on flower bed.

11. Scrub porch with hot soapy water.

12. Turn tubs upside down.

13. Go put on cleen dress—smooth hair with side combs—brew a cup of tee—set and rest and rock a spell and count blessins.

See this woman's pride. Note her accomplishments. Appreciate her reasonable plan and pace. She never needed a psychiatrist because of the stress of overcommitment. She just did what needed to be done, and she enjoyed the results.

Is there an equivalent in your life? Is there a job you can do with your hands? Is there a bending and stretching and aerobic workout awaiting you in your own home? Maybe you could eliminate harried trips to the health club if you just embraced your "home" work. And maybe doing so would surprise you with simple joy.

I catch rainwater in a barrel. I love dipping a small bucket into it and watering the flowers or even washing my hair in it. I peel peaches on the porch swing. I iron near a window over-looking the flower garden. In these times I catch elusive day-dreams before they run away, and I've experienced the joy of planning, executing, and completing a task.

Think about women of previous generations—perhaps your own grandmother or great-grandmother. She had no alarm to ring her awake, no boss to please, no deadlines except those she set. Her home was her job and her joy. She was pro-prietor, initiator, decorator, manager, chef, hostess, and project manager of her domain.

Is there a work you can borrow from great-grandma's day to recapture the joy of work at home? Can you hang a few clothes on a rack in the sun for the pure pleasure of seeing the warm light whiten them before your eyes? Can you polish an antique desk with loving vigor until it gleams like it hasn't in years?

God gave you and me our daily lives for purposeful plea-sure, not just for relentless activity that grinds us down. Go, then. Find a work you can do with pleasure and satisfaction. Wash some windows until they sparkle. Polish some silver until it gleams. Refinish a battered chest of drawers and watch its original beauty emerge. Embrace the joys at home.

God, I wonder why I always think somewhere else is "where it's at." I mean, why do I have to go away to find satisfaction and fulfillment? When I think about it, home could be where I can find the joy of accomplishment, the contentment that comes with a job completed well...at least part of the time.

Home. Maybe I haven't spent enough time thinking about it in this light, God, or making it as nurturing as it can be. But I'm drawn to the idea. What do you think? Shall we walk around and get some ideas together?

If I've rushed past simple joys in my own home, no wonder I'm feeling some emptiness. If I need a change of perspective, renew a right spirit within me. Lord, give me the ability to find joy in the simple process of being and working at home.

"I pass a lot of houses on my way home.
Some pretty, some expensive, some inviting.
But my heart always skips a beat
when I turn down the road and see
my house nestled against the hill."

—BOB BENSON

Create Something "Unnecessary"

Creativity is as old as God. It flows from God. It is who he is. When we create, we are not merely expressing a skill or a talent, but we are displaying a grand exhibition of our deep and eternal connection to our Creator.

So to me it's no surprise that I frequently have the urge to create, and I suspect you do too if you pay attention to what comes naturally. The urge to be creative is one we shouldn't resist because our creativity is one way God expresses himself in the world through us. I don't know about you, but that excites me! If we are warehousing even a tiny fragment of God's creativity, he will surely give us limitless opportunities to express it.

So let yourself look within. Where do you see the stamp of the Creator in you? Do you have an urge to design, build, paint, sculpt, arrange, compose, write, cook, invent? Then now is your time to do it—or at least to allow yourself a half-hour to begin a project. The very fact that you're doing something "unnecessary," just for the joy of it, will be freeing and refreshing. From the well of your own inner resources and interests you will draw ideas that can become realities. Are you ready to begin?

Let yourself be whimsical…playful. Design a new hairdo for yourself. Pick a bouquet from your garden and arrange it in an antique teapot. Wrap a pretty piece of fabric around an old couch cushion and brighten your sofa. Whittle on a stick or compose a simple tune. It doesn't matter what you do. It matters only that you listen to and follow the urge of the original Creator by doing something of your own. Creating, by its very nature, will refresh and heal you.

Make this time the "glad hallelujah" of your week. Determine not to answer your phone or interrupt your interlude to put in another load of laundry. Relax any compulsion to explain or justify this time to inquisitive relatives or friends. Don't feel you have to tell someone why you're not "working."

"No matter how good your intentions may be, no woman can handle the stress of managing [her life] when she has not given herself vital opportunity for essential refueling."

—S H A R O N H O F F M A N

You might want to dabble with your cosmetics. Cut off the tip ends of two lipsticks, press them into a small dish, and come up with a new color. Press this mixture into an empty lipstick or blush container and apply with your finger or a sponge. Add a little petroleum jelly and you have lip gloss…enough for a year!

Glue some antique buttons on earring backs purchased from a craft store. Paint your fingernails and toenails a scrumptious new shade. Attend an art or dance or gourmet cooking class. Your choices are endless. I knew a woman who picked up the smooth stones outside her door and began painting on them and selling them in local art stores. My husband took wooden shingles from one-hundred-year-old barns and built tiny barn replicas from them.

Possibility is where we all dwell because the Originator of all possibilities dwells within us! When we allow the "necessary" and urgent to consistently stomp out the inspiration and time to create, we shrivel something that was meant to blossom. Whenever the drive to go and to get and to add supersedes the impulse to make, we have probably followed our culture too closely and our Christ from too far away.

You may look at your life, throw up your hands, and exclaim, "Who has time to create?!" But consider, with that very question you are admitting a natural urge and the desire to honor it. So…do. Your God-instilled desire to create will never go away, you know. Not even if you stuff it, rebuff it, ignore it, or starve it. We women today are experts at sublimating our feminine desires and creative impulses. But we are made in the image of God, so he will keep "coming out." We will always have the inclination to be the originator of something.

The main thing to remember is this: For this interlude of creative time you've set apart, you are not maintaining, keeping up with, cleaning, organizing, rearranging, repairing, washing, delivering, attending to, listening for, studying, earning, managing, buying, selling, teaching, or driving. When your interlude is over, you will be surprised at the new energy you feel.

And when we're ninety, will we look back and wish we had worked more and been more productive in society's eyes? I think not. Will we wish we had enjoyed life more and played and created more along the way? I'm sure of it. So, my friend, give in to the urge to do something creative. Let this be a time of divine infilling as you open yourself to the Creator God who joyfully allows his exquisite goodness to flow through you. If you collaborate with your limitless Creator, whatever comes out will be a bit of God and, as such, holy.

My Creator God…is it really true? Are you and I that much alike? Am I a reflection of you? And is taking time to create an okay occupation? Then where did I get the idea I'm not acceptable if I don't work or serve or minister my life away?

I think I'm hearing that faint knocking inside my soul that says, "Do it now! Express what's inside today, while there is still today." I'm listening.

You know, Lord, when I slow down and just sit with you for a while, these desires to create come to the surface. It's as if they're down there bubbling all the time, waiting for an outlet. Mostly what I see when I slow down is how often I have ignored your divine permission to wrap my arms around life and dance a jig with it.

Oh yes, this is the glad hallelujah of my week! And it won't be the last time I'll do something "unnecessary." Lord of all creation, thank you for making me in your image and giving me joy in the act—even in the thought—of creating something of my own.

"The kind of simple life you've dreamed about,
longed for, sought out...it really can be
as wonderful as you've imagined it.
All you have to do is choose it...now."

—THOMAS KINKADE

Then I realized that it is good and proper for a man to eat and drink, and to find satisfaction in his toilsome labor under the sun during the few days of life God has given him.

ECCLESIASTES 5:18

Take Yourself Out to Lunch

Savor an elegant lunch just for one. You can and you should. Whether you choose a spot with white linen or a lovely old wood table, order a lunch fit for a queen and enjoy it royally.

Find an eatery that offers a pleasing view or cloistered privacy, according to your mood. Choose a place with music and food to your liking. Take along a favorite book if you feel uncomfortable eating alone.

When you've chosen your place, dress for the occasion. Add a colorful scarf or a pretty pin or your favorite hat—something that will help you designate this time as personal and out of the ordinary.

Take your time studying the menu. Select something nourishing, but delightful to your taste buds and pleasing to your eyes. When your meal arrives, take delight in the fragrance and the color of the food before you even lift your fork. Don't hurry through your meal so you can get on with other things. Dawdle a little. This is your time to nourish both body and soul. Lean back in your seat and allow your senses to take in the whole of this experience. You are, blessedly, alone. Someone will cater to your needs. Another will cook and yet another will clear your table. For this brief hour, shed all responsibility and enjoy the remarkable and singular joys of honoring yourself with a dining experience. Become fully present to the moment, intentionally enjoying every aspect of this luncheon for one.

You, who have been giving yourself away in driblets to those around you, are regathered and restored. Your table is your sanctuary, and this hour a gift you give yourself. Here, in this treasured hour, your heart rises in gratitude for the joy of just being alive and able to enjoy life's simple pleasures. So simple a thing—just to treat yourself to lunch. Why haven't you done it before…or more often? Note what you have missed and ask "why?" Think seriously about the ease with which you sometimes give away the same money and time to those who hardly notice.

"We can go to great lengths (or at least a two-hour drive) to keep daily life from smothering the soul. But as you do, you can re-collect a scattered life and focus on the one who calls and seeks and invites us to communion."

—PHILIP ZALESKI

One fall day when I was working hard to meet a deadline, I took a break from my studio and headed for the nearest hamlet. Recently emptied of tourists, the streets seemed to especially embrace old friends, and the restaurant was a step into another world. The fireplace, the ferns, the paintings—all conspired to seduce me into far more than a mere cup of coffee. I stayed. I ate a delightful meal. And eventually, because of this refreshing hour, I wrote again…newly empowered by an interlude just for me.

"Four dollars and fifty cents," the cashier said as I paid my bill. That was the full cost of an interlude of stunning significance! Such a small price for peace and renewed strength. Minimum charge for magic.

Lord, I marvel at how much you provide for me throughout the day. You are here…there…everywhere. In the restaurant, you were there. On the street, you were there. In the changing leaves I saw you. Did you enjoy my joy? Oh, I think you did! We are partners in this thing called life, and you will never, ever leave me. Boy, am I glad!

Lord, help me never to become adept at saying no to small pleasures. Help me to develop a childlike heart that anticipates joy around every corner and leaps boldly toward and into it with sheer delight and total abandon. Teach me how to skip and run gladheartedly through your world with arms outstretched to receive your abundant blessings. Be my guide and mentor in keeping a springlike attitude, fresh and unsullied by my culture's incessant demands, because my eyes are on you, the Author and Finisher of my faith.

"If you don't want to die of thirst in the desert of this world, let your soul drink of God's love."

—ALEXANDRA STODDARD

Browse in a Bookshop

If books have become your friends, as they have mine, a visit to a bookshop will be like visiting an old friend, one you've known for years. And if a good friend is a lot like a soft pillow, a visit to a bookshop will be a lot like a romp on a feather bed!

Dress for the occasion. Wear your favorite or most fun or most comfortable outfit. A visit like this may call for a special accessory or a perky hat. Take a large tote bag because you may return home with an armload of treasures. Set out with a sense of adventure. After all, you never know who or what you will meet between the covers of a book!

Where is your favorite bookstore? Go there if you can. Or go in search of a shop tucked away, off the beaten path. Find one that smells of books and leather and dust. Find one whose owner loves books and loves to talk about them. Look for one with a reading corner, where you can tuck your feet underneath you and browse at length before making up your mind what you like or what you might want to buy. I'm thinking of a favorite bookshop of mine where I can sit in an old wicker rocker overlooking a lake, with the owner's dog lying quietly at my feet.

> *"Different people can find their privacy and seclusion in different places. There are all kinds of 'prayer closets.'"*
>
> —PHILLIP KELLER

Seek out some of the very oldest of books, for in them are forgotten ways, customs, manners, fashions. In them, you can discover what it was like to live and work and breathe more slowly in another era. Dip into a children's classic, like *Heidi,* and find yourself breathing the pristine air of the Alps, eating cheese and bread, and drinking goat's milk. Wander a bit from your usual interests in order to stretch your mind. You might even choose a subject to explore for the year and revisit often with an air of expectation.

When you're finished browsing and have purchased a new or used treasure (or ten!), go to a quiet little restaurant or coffee shop. Order a cup of steaming coffee or tea. Then dip into one of your new literary finds just enough to taste it so you will be tempted back into it at another time that calls for an interlude of restful reflection.

Do you wonder how God feels about a bookshop outing? Well, isn't he the inspiration behind many books? The source of strength you have to go there? The provider of the car or bicycle that takes you there? Yes! Our God enjoys seeing his children at play. He loves to play along with us! So don't forget to take him with you on your excursion.

Go, then. Make your way among the books and meet them as you would good friends. In a bookshop, all the cantankerous voices calling you to busyness are silenced.

Lord, this is an unusual way to slow down. Being so purposeful about doing something for myself goes against the grain. It seems a little selfish and self-absorbed. But I'm willing to give it a try. I have nothing to lose, I suppose. So I'll do it and see what happens. Maybe it'll be a little like taking a mental vacation. All those annoying thoughts bumping around in my head will have to move over and make room for something fresh. Maybe it will work.

A mental vacation…now that sounds good, Lord. For a brief time I can live by faith, believing that you are taking care of things without my vigilant attention. And maybe this gentle interlude will be the beginning of a larger faith that knows at all times that you are lovingly in charge.

Books: the lives and thoughts of others preserved for me…just waiting to jostle my thinking and enlarge my mental territory. As the proverb says, "As iron sharpens iron, so one man sharpens another." Well then, I welcome the thoughts in these books because surely my mind needs sharpening.

Come along with me, Lord. Help me select just the books that will feed my soul and expand my mind. And most of all, help me to simply enjoy your quiet companionship.

---

*"If women were convinced that a day off
or an hour of solitude was a reasonable ambition,
they would find a way of attaining it."*

—ANNE MORROW LINDBERGH

*Be still before the LORD
and wait patiently for him.*

PSALM 37:7

Dawdle on Purpose

How long has it been since you lingered instead of rushed? How long since you dawdled on purpose over a satisfying meal or even a cup of coffee?

When anything wonderful is coming to an end, I tend to linger. I don't want it to go away. And when time slips through my fingers and disappears like grains of sand, I pause just long enough to let memories imprint themselves on my heart. At such times, I feel the enjoyment of the experience pour over me again even as it is being transformed into a memory and stored for future pleasure.

This morning, I dallied over breakfast at a favorite restaurant. My window seat overlooked a brook, and fresh flowers were a grace note on my table. Music drifted lazily throughout the room, and savory food gave me pleasure. When the plate was empty, I looked for an excuse to linger. "Coffee?" my server asked. "Of course."

Then there was the day my daughter left for California. She was leaving in moments, and she would be gone for years.

We dawdled, we fumbled, we hugged, we cried, we lingered: Devoid of words, we hoped somehow to delay the inevitable. The moments somehow passed, and she boarded the plane. Left behind, I paused on the spot where she stood just moments before, still engaged by her presence.

Blooming flower beds are a perfect excuse for dawdling. Do a little sniffing, a little touching. Look ever so closely at each blossom and consider with awe the velvety perfection. If only each petal would remain forever at its peak! But it won't, and that's a good enough reason to linger.

Letters from loved ones deserve some quality lingering too. Some call for two or more readings because they bring such pleasure. I like to sit on my porch swing with a glass of sparkling water and meander through a fine letter a second or even a third time, savoring each thought.

You might try lingering over creativity in its many forms, whether in a storefront display or a painting or a one-of-a-kind sculpture. I've found that the creations of others stimulate my own creativity. Even a woman who dresses artfully, combining shape and texture and cut and color, is inspiring to me. Or notice the man who wears his cowboy hat at just the right angle. Even that is worth a moment's dawdling appreciation. A beautifully appointed table is artistry to be honored. A quilted throw artfully draped over a chair arm is worth admiring at leisure.

And shouldn't we linger over such things as ice-cream cones? And kisses? Sunsets? Hot cups of cocoa? To do so, I believe, is to consciously and gratefully acknowledge the multitude of pleasantries that grace our lives. It is to notice the steppingstones God has placed along our pathways to enhance and adorn our days.

> *"Most people I know repeatedly make one or two basic choices that keep their lives out of control and leave them feeling chronically rushed and dissatisfied."*
>
> —THOMAS KINKADE

Why not choose to go from steppingstone to steppingstone during this hour, lingering a bit longer than necessary over gossamer moments? After all, they are the embellishments of your life and help you to enjoy each day as it unfolds.

Even prayer can be a kind of holy dawdling in the presence of God, for when you pray, you are renewed at your core by the power of God's Spirit. So consider quietly lingering in the presence of the Lord, not worrying about whether you have read scripture or officially prayed. There's something about tarrying with God that pulls the garment of intimacy around you both.

In church I am often deeply moved and long to linger in God's presence. You, too, may recall times of corporate worship as you sang, the praise notes seeming to float in the sanctuary even after the singing stopped. At those times, the Holy Spirit walks strongly among us, and we recognize a holy longing to encapsulate the joy and be cleansed by the sparkling luminescence of the moment. Such times are a rite of triumphal passage for God and his people, and must never be hurried.

When you can, find any excuse to linger awhile. Linger at a beautiful place. Discover a scenic spot and simply stay awhile, admiring the sublime and the extraordinary, being captivated by the splendor. It is necessary, you know, to occasionally saturate your soul with beauty lest your life be reduced to a list of accomplishments. Don't let that happen. Dawdle on purpose, to the glory of God.

Lord, help me linger over the gossamer moments that grace my daily path. Sometimes I'm rushing around so much I can't even recognize them, let alone linger over them. It seems as if I've been rushing from one thing to another since I was a child, so dawdling doesn't come easy. In fact, I've seen it as something of a character weakness in others. An American woman dawdling? The very idea almost makes me laugh. But when I think about it, those who know how to linger are the very people who seem to have sunbeams wound through their hair, who laugh a lot, and who begin each day as a new adventure.

I'm sorry, Lord, but you'll need to completely reeducate me if I'm ever to learn this lesson. Besides, how in the world will it fit in with multitasking? "Not at all," you say? But what about…?

All right, God, I'm willing to learn. And dare I admit: The whole concept sounds *wonderful!*

I think I especially need to dawdle in your presence. My typical routine doesn't work very well. You know: I rush into your presence, set the clock for ten minutes or so, and rush away again. Sometimes my holy time with you is nothing more than something to check off my list. No wonder my life remains unchanged. Restrain me, Lord. Strap me to my chair if you have to! Put blinders on me so I can see only you in all your majesty!

Thank you for your infinite patience with me, a slow learner. But you know, somehow I think it's okay to be slow today.

"Hurry is not just a disordered schedule,
hurry is a disordered heart."

—JOHN ORTBERG

Meditate in an Empty Church

Is there a certain church sanctuary that strongly appeals to you? It may not even be your own church, but one you have visited or have always wanted to see inside. You may have pictured yourself just sitting for a while in this quiet, lovely place, in the soothing presence of God.

Just the thought of spending an extended period of such tranquillity in a treasured place may have long charmed you, but you've brushed the idea aside as something you'll do some-day—maybe.

Let today be your day to go! Go, and for an hour just sit in reflection and prayer and worship. Meet the God who promises to renew your strength.

Choose a time that will be uninterrupted by a cleaning crew or groups of people. You might call the church secretary and ask her to recommend a time for your interlude. Most churches will welcome you to "come away" and will honor your desire to be left alone once you arrive.

Early in the morning, at dawn, might be the best time for you. Or, going right in the middle of a busy day, when the world is running crazily around you may be the most meaningful. Whatever the time you choose, go to this special place and sit in silence. Take only yourself. No books, journal, music. Nothing. This hour will be an exercise in resting your soul, in leaning into the peace to be found in the presence of the living God.

I know a woman who has made this her daily practice for eighteen years: She spends an hour of silence in a church on her way to work as a teacher. Is it any wonder that her life spreads out like an oak tree covering her students with godly compassion, wise instruction, and keen understanding?

"We have only ourselves to blame if we turn from God, occupying ourselves instead with the trifles of life."

—BROTHER LAWRENCE

You might begin your own time of meditation by placing each distracting thought in God's hands. Talk over your worries with the Lord rather than pushing them down or feeling annoyed by them. They are messages from your soul and deserve to be attended to. After a time you will find yourself wanting to hear from God, and you will become more still.

Just wait. Allow him time to speak to your soul and clarify your thoughts.

Don't be anxious if you seem to hear nothing at first. Listening is a learned skill that will not come quickly or easily in the beginning. You may have to forcefully render yourself speechless and teach your mind to subject to the authority of quietness its desire to chatter.

So, just wait. You probably won't realize the good being done to your innermost being until some time later. You may need to visit a church often before noticing any heart changes. Over time, however, this kind of communion with God will produce a spirit more calm and sure than you ever dreamed possible. There is enormous power in stillness when that stillness is focused on the Master of the universe.

So you may want to devote one hour each week to this quietness in place of your regular devotional pattern. Come to the sanctuary knowing that God may change you in unexpected ways, but don't make a plan and expect him to follow it. Experiment with taking your hands off even your devotional life and simply spending a quiet hour of love with your Creator. Let him decide what will happen. Let him chart your course and determine your mode of travel. He knows best what needs to happen in your soul.

If it helps, think of this interlude as a date with God. Then, think of the way you've prepared for dates that were important to you and how eager you were to be with the one you loved.

Remember how time with that person was always too short. And remember that it didn't matter what you did, but only that you were together, giving and receiving love. Sometimes this being together occurred in silence; at other times there were words.

So it will be with God. Now giving, now receiving, but mostly abiding…listening…waiting—the best-kept secrets of spiritual power.

Here I am, Lord. I never thought I could sit still like this without making a lot of prayer noise or hearing a lot of mental clatter. If I'm fidgety, I hope you'll overlook that because sitting still is hardly natural for me. It goes against almost everything I've done or heard of doing. There's that word again: *do.* I can't seem to get rid of it. But then, I was born in America and I'm a woman on the go. See how I'm chattering even as I begin! Why do I always think I have to fill in the silences as if you couldn't think of a thing to say!

It's so quiet here…so still. I know you aren't exclusively or even especially in a church, Lord, but being here helps me to sense your presence. I feel your permission to slouch down a bit and let go and be truly myself. I might as well because you know me anyway. So here I am, palms up and heart open. I'm ready to receive whatever you have to give or to listen to whatever you have to say. I just want to be with you and experience you without distraction.

And to prove it, I'm going to hush my mind right now and wait on you. For in your presence, there is healing…there is power…there is love. And that's what I need.

"Be silent and listen to God. Let your heart be in such a state of preparation that His Spirit may impress upon you such virtues as will please Him. Let all within you listen to Him."

—FRANÇOIS FÉNELON

I remember the days of long ago;
I meditate on all your works
and consider what your hands have done.

PSALM 143:5

Visit Memory Lane

Memories. Some we cherish; others we wish we could forget. But remembering, even the difficult times, is almost always a beneficial exercise for the heart, especially if we look back and see God standing in the shadows of every experience.

Often remembering forges the courage in us to move ahead: We've looked back and been reminded of how far we've come. Remembering also has a way of giving us a stronger sense of place—of where we belong today, why we are here, and which direction God wants us to go next. Memories help us to appreciate the roles various people have played in our lives—ways they chose to live, how their choices affected them and us and others, how God ordered their steps, and how we can make better choices today because of lessons we learned from them.

Sometimes, when my love for life, my affection and tolerance for people, and my intimacy with God grow dim, a visit to memory lane restores my soul and realigns my vision. When I visit the past, whether the journey takes me to joyful moments or bittersweet times, I am inevitably struck by God's faithfulness to ultimately work for my good in all things (Romans 8:28).

"We want not to miss God's whispers amid the noisy clutter."
—TIMOTHY JONES

Besides, visiting memory lane is often just plain fun! Especially if you are privileged, as I have been, to have a walk-in attic or a similar place for reminiscing. In an attic, wonderment abounds! Lovers' secrets are hidden in beribboned letters. Faded dresses and old-fashioned hats hint at adventures gone by. Photos and paintings and odd bits of the past hide in dusty trunks, beckoning to be revisited and relished. To step through the door of my attic is to leave the present entirely and to enter the past with all its regalia, its stories, its wisdom, and its vigor.

We all need to visit memory lane occasionally because history, especially family history, gives dimension and perspective to our present. So spend this hour wandering through the relics of your past. Go to an attic or a basement. Curl up with a photo album or a scrapbook. Give yourself the time to really settle in, then begin to turn the pages of yesterday and yesteryear. Smile at beloved faces and speak to those now missing. Hug a baby in your mind, recall a riveting experience, renew a vow, reexperience emotions almost forgotten. Laugh. Cry. Pray. And thank God for walking alongside you through both good and bad.

Remembering will feed your soul. It will inspire you to leave footprints for others to follow. And you will not regret what is not accomplished while you're meditating on all God has done—in you and through you and in spite of you. It will be an hour well spent.

Everlasting God, you dwell even among memories! You amaze me, astound me. If I go up into the highest heaven, you're there. If I dig into the depths of the earth, or scratch around in musty memories, you're there too! I feel the passion and the affection for me flowing from your heart.

Lord, I look at fragments of the past and the lives people have lived, and a word comes to mind: *legacies.* They have left legacies. In one way or another, they have influenced not only their own generation, but mine…and me. Their lives have not been silent or gone unnoticed.

As I live my own life, God, go ahead of me and clear out the brush so I, too, can leave a good and lasting legacy that points people to you. I want to avoid the mistakes I've witnessed and not repeat those that I've lived. I want the memories I leave to be good ones…to have your fingerprints all over them.

"The God who spoke in times past still speaks
and will continue to speak throughout history."

—JOYCE HUGGETT

O LORD, you have searched me and you know me.
You know when I sit and when I rise;
you perceive my thoughts from afar.

PSALM 139:1-2

Dare to Dream

Louisa May Alcott, famed author of *Little Women,* said, "A little kingdom I possess where thoughts and feelings dwell." She was speaking of the place, way down deep inside us all, where we think and feel and dream.

I believe that inside every woman is a place where day-dreams long to stretch out and grow into possibilities, into realities. I know one woman who says that, for all the years of her self-reflective life, she has hankered for a place to foster day-dreams, one molded to her own liking. That place finally presented itself to her in a little building on her property. "It stands a ways back from the big house," she says. "Just close enough to run back, just in case."

We all need such a place for dreaming, and we can create one wherever we happen to be. I intend to build one today in a public park I love. There I will let myself dream beside a wide, flowing river with a fountain gushing from its center, park benches scattered along its perimeter, and a walkway and bridge to feed the contemplative part of my heart.

"Our four-poster bed is high off the floor, and when I sit up straight, comforted by several pillows, I'm free to gaze out at the water. Only in solitude are we able to daydream."

—ALEXANDRA STODDARD

To dream is to let go of what must be and what is. It is to step out, far into the land of wishes and deepest desires, and to dare to hold them, as one would a precious jewel, if only for a moment. It is to free fall into the vortex of "maybes" and "why nots." It is to play—to free possibilities that have been buried by obligation and tedious living. Most women no longer intentionally dream, it seems, because dreaming is viewed by many as an accident to be corrected or a flaw to repair or even a waste of time. A wandering mind—do you dare?

Today, for this hour, you do! Let yourself imagine where you have always wanted to live. Paint a picture of it in your mind. What color is the roof? The siding? How will you decorate the interior, and what do you want the house to say about those who live inside? Where will this home, or home-away-from-home, be located, and what will you be able to see when you step up to the front window? What friends will enter and be nourished in these surroundings? Go ahead. Build a house in your dreams. You may derive as much pleasure as if you owned it this moment.

What have you always wanted to do? What dream lies dormant, waiting for the right time? Do you want to play an instrument? Learn to dance? Design an interior? Travel the world? Meet someone famous? Adopt a child? Run a bed-and-breakfast inn? Write a book? All of us have such dreams, and it is good to pull them out and mull them over, not only for the pleasure of it, but also because God is often the originator of our dreams.

Talk your dreams over with God and then put them into his hands for safekeeping and development in his perfect time. As you get in the habit of talking with God about your secret dreams, some may evaporate. Others may settle in permanently, becoming his calling on your life. Yes, dreams are often transformed into settled hopes and, eventually, realities.

In our culture today, we devise our plans, muster up our own resources, and take specific steps to reach our predetermined objectives. We make the dream happen by ourselves. But I like to think that the dreams God puts in our hearts are the very ones we feel totally incapable of reaching. They take faith. And if they do come true, his miraculous power and love will be evident in it all. Dreams that are born in our quiet interludes with God require his sovereign design and continual intervention—and have everlasting results.

We all dream. Dreaming is the starting point for a divine-human cooperative to accomplish God's goals on earth. God plants dreams in people's hearts and then comes alongside to make them come true.

Go, then, to a place of daydreams, a place of possibilities, and set your dreams free. Dream as you walk barefoot beside an ocean, salt breezes ruffling your garments. Dream as you lie in bed in the darkness. Dream as you drive in the country where traffic can't distract you. Dream as you do mindless work. Dream as you slide into a warm bath and watch a candle flicker in the shadows. Dream on a porch swing, in a garden, in a library, a church, or an art gallery.

Your dreams are your own. They belong to you. They need not be shared except with God. They live in your innermost sanctuary, where your heart's treasures are kept. Most are locked away too long and become dusty and dull. But your dreams need not be. Take them out now, sense the joy of their possibilities, feel them pull you into the future with a shade more anticipation than you have without them.

The woman who is free to dream cannot easily be held hostage to unpleasant circumstances. She soars above them and beyond them, and she brings to her daily life a sound hope and an insistent spirit that proclaim freedom and new possibilities. And she always, always finds a lighted pathway through even the darkest of nights.

Lord, it's me. I'm going to take this old dream out of my pocket now and look it over. It's been in there too long. I want to know what you think about it. This seems scary, maybe even a little childish. I can think of a million reasons why I shouldn't even look at this. But what do you think?

I don't know where this dream came from, Lord, but it has been there for a long time. It seems impossible. It seems illogical. Yet it's there, and it won't be dislodged. You say that with you, nothing is impossible, and I think I believe it. Yet when I take this dream out and dust it off, I see only impossibilities and obstacles.

Lord, if this dream came from you, and if you really are in the business of giving us the desires of our hearts, then will you take this precious jewel from my hands and keep it safe while you position me to receive it back, for your glory? I've tried to make this dream come true on my own, but it hasn't…and I can't. And I guess that's good, because you're the worker of miracles—and I need one.

So here, Lord, take it, all my dream stuff. And I'll wait in eager expectation to see what you're going to do.

---

*"I would rather live in a world where my life
is surrounded by mystery
than live in a world so small
that my mind could comprehend it."*

—HARRY EMERSON FOSDICK

The LORD is my shepherd,
I shall not be in want.

PSALM 23:1

Spend an Hour
with God

Does an hour spent with God seem like a long time? Is it hard for you to imagine what you would say in the presence of the Almighty? If your answer is yes, then you are in good company!

Maybe it will help to remember a few things before you begin. First, God made you. He understands you. He always has your best interests in mind. He enjoys you! He forgives you upon request. He listens without condemnation. You can tell him anything, anywhere, anytime, anyplace, any way. He is utterly approachable. Everything good that could be written is true of God. And because he accepts you exactly where you are at the moment, you can entirely relax in his presence.

If you have found a quiet spot and are seated comfortably, or even if you are walking at a leisurely pace, you are ready to commune with the divine. Most call this prayer. I call it simple conversation with my best friend.

May I suggest just one of many structures you could use for

your hour with God? Use just five words for this hour. As you take your time with each word, you will discover the transforming power of truth.

God gave us Psalm 23 through his servant David. Now, you are going to give it back to God, thoughtfully and in faith. Take one word at a time and extract the full meaning from it. Talk each word over with God. As you meditate on each word, you will find that any temporary estrangement from God will be reconciled. And by the end of your hour, God will have done a good work in your heart.

You can choose any small portion of scripture on which to meditate, word by word. But for the first time you spend an hour interlude with God, try praying through the first verse of Psalm 23 and learn a simple way to draw your heart close to his.

The Lord… "What a wonderful word! My soul waits for a word from you, Lord. You are indeed Master of the universe. You are the final authority in my life. You have the last word: not me, not my culture. Lord, help me see where I have been my own master and followed the dictates of others without even consulting you. Forgive me! Restore me!"

Is… "Right now, at this very moment, you are Lord, aren't you? Right here, in this very place, you're my Shepherd. Present tense. Yesterday, today, and forever, you are alive and intensely interested in me. I receive your attention and tenderhearted love and feel it flowing through my spirit. You are present beside me, within me, all around me. In every moment of every day, you are here. Thank you, Lord!"

My… "O Dear God, you belong to me! You are mine! You have pledged yourself to me. And I am yours. You aren't merely the God of pastors or churches or theologians, but of the common person…of me. You have stooped to touch my life and unveiled your magnificent heart to me in scripture. You want to be my Lord, yet I know you to be the God who won't push any farther than I allow. You wait for me to invite you in, to welcome you in humble adoration. Ah, Lord, welcome to my humble heart."

Shepherd… "With infinite attention and diligent care, you see to my every need. You watch my coming and my going, my lying down and my sitting up. You nurture and guide me even when I don't realize it or appreciate it. You are Shepherd of my soul—what a comforting truth! You care for me when I can't care for myself. You know when I stray from the fold, and you are willing to give your very life to bring me back safely. Good shepherd, I'm so glad you always come after me."

> *"Meditative prayer creates the emotional and spiritual space which allows Christ to construct an inner sanctuary in the heart."*
>
> —RICHARD FOSTER

These prayer-words are mine, and if they help you in your hour, I'm delighted. But *your* words are precious to God. Whether or not you can even speak above a whisper or know good grammar, he values your unique way of talking to him. Whatever words you use, he reads your heart like an open book, and savors it.

So take an hour and open your heart to the Shepherd, who seeks only your good. Tell him your intimate thoughts. Sink deep into the truth that the Lord is your Shepherd. Allow him to tend to your soul. He waits to change the course of your day, even of your life, forever.

Precious Shepherd! I'd forgotten what an hour with you was like! At last, for this little while, you've turned my focus inward and, more important, upward. I've stopped long enough to really appreciate who you are, and I can't explain what that does for me. Your bigness confounds me. I'm diminished by it, yet made stronger. My problems shrink, and my soul grows.

As Saint Augustine once said, "You breathed your fragrance upon me, and in astonishment I drew my breath. Now I pant for you! I tasted you, and now I hunger and thirst for you." That's so true, Lord. More of you makes me hungry and thirsty for more of you. Yet how you satisfy! This hour of pure adoration and worship somehow straightens all the pictures on the wall of my life.

Draw me here again, Lord…and again! For here, I am changed. In only an hour.

"We can get so fearfully busy trying to carry out the second greatest commandment, 'Thou shalt love thy neighbor as thyself,' that we are underdeveloped in our devoted love to God."

—Thomas R. Kelly

Trade Houses with a Friend

Do you ever need a change of scenery? Even if you're gone from home all day or home is your workplace, do you still find it refreshing to visit the home of another? Ahhh! All the responsibility is lifted from your shoulders, and you relax more fully. Even the food is tastier! And it just doesn't matter if there's dust on someone else's furniture.

If a change of scenery sounds good to you, then you might want to consider trading houses with a friend for a day. I do this on a regular basis with an acquaintance who simply wants to change her scenery when she spends a special day alone with God. We both feel freer in someone else's home to relax our bodies and souls and to get God's perspective on our lives. We don't look around and see what needs repairing or adjusting or cleaning or changing. Spending the day in a different environment is like turning to a new page in a notebook: fresh, unsullied, blank. In someone else's house our hands and hearts are emptied of "musts" and "shoulds," and so it's much easier to pray and to read and to release our concerns.

One friend spent a whole day on my front porch and said her life has never been the same. Since then, she has been referring others to "Linda's front porch"—and they have been coming! In God's hands a simple porch is a place of rest and transformation.

"I believe you must regularly get away from people."

—ALEXANDRA STODDARD

If you're going away on vacation, why not loan your home to a friend or acquaintance who really needs some time alone? This solitude can be just what God needs to do his work in a hungry heart. Instead of sitting empty and useless, your home can be used as a meeting place for God and one of his children.

On one of our weekends away, a woman stayed in our home overnight because she needed time to plan a speech. She had no family at home, but she needed a change of scenery. Her retreat cost neither of us anything, and it benefited us both. Two other women I know, with thirteen children between them, spent a day in the empty home of a friend. They had quality conversation, tears, tea, and prayer in a way they never could have had they not been gifted with that space.

Everybody's schedules are different, but usually we can make time to get away. If you don't feel you can take a whole day, then maybe a couple of hours to call your own will do the trick. Perhaps you can explore this "trading houses" idea by first offering your home for a few hours to someone you know and trust. If that becomes comfortable, move on to trying an "exchange" day. Wave as you pass your friend on your way to each other's houses. And when you arrive, pray for your friend. Then give yourself with abandon to the new space you have craved and now can enjoy.

Each generation offers unique possibilities for ministering to others as well as caring for our own souls. Trading houses for an hour or a day is an idea beginning to surface as a plausible, affordable way to retreat. I have found that loaning out my home and spending time in someone else's is a remarkably easy and powerful way to nurture a more restful heart, both in myself and in someone else. In someone else's home, you aren't compelled to work. You simply don't see the dust. And if you do, you aren't responsible. You can rest. If having this kind of soul space appeals to you, I know you will find a way. And it may open delightful new doors you never dreamed of!

Lord, you are so utterly creative and dynamic. Even if I can't do it now, this idea opens possibilities I long to explore. When I think about it, there are empty homes everywhere I look, homes being used for nothing most of the time.

Right now, I'm thinking about a time my own home will be empty. Why not let ———— stay for a day or invite ———— to bring her girls for a special mom/daughter sleepover? Why not offer to let ———— and ———— come spend a day together? It could be just what they need as individuals and as friends—women longing both for rest and for more of you. Then there's the minister and his wife—they haven't had a free getaway in so long. Maybe here! Maybe then! They don't want luxury. They just want peace, solitude, and quiet.

O Lord, I sense this whole idea of loaning and trading houses has your approval. It's something you would do. What a simple way to share with others what you've given me. And what a terrific way to find rest for my own too-busy hands and heart.

"The emotional depletion that results
from living in a crisis mode
eventually produces a shrinking heart."

—BILL AND LYNNE HYBELS

You have made known to me the path of life;
you will fill me with joy in your presence,
with eternal pleasures at your right hand.

PSALM 16:11

Take a DAWG Day

Because of the nature of a woman's busy life, she spills herself away in tributaries all day, day after day, week after week. If she is to thrive and continue to nurture others, she must replenish her own river of life.

A few years ago, our minister suggested we spend a whole day with God every so often, for the purpose of realigning, reordering, and refilling our lives. He recommended doing so once a month, which was his practice. I took the challenge, and have been spending between three hours and one full day every month on a DAWG day—a Day Alone With God.

What is a DAWG day? And how do you do it? Well, it's very simple. Let me give you a dozen suggestions and ask you to try it—at least once. When you do, you probably won't hesitate to do it again!

1. Pick a day, or at least a few hours, to be alone. In fact, pick twelve days (one for each month) and mark them in ink on your calendar.

2. Before each DAWG day arrives, find a place conducive to quiet contemplation and prayer.

3. Take only a Bible, a notebook dedicated to your DAWG days, and a favorite pen. You'll keep this notebook as a record of what God does in your heart on these special days set apart just for you and him.

4. As you begin your day, write out all the problems you currently struggle with and all the questions and concerns you have about them.

5. Talk each one over with God, asking him to give you direction and answers and insight as you move through the day. Don't demand immediate answers, but begin simply to listen.

6. Consider dividing your life into categories (for example: Personal, Occupational, Relational, Physical, Spiritual). Review each area with God, asking him to tell you what needs to be adjusted, what to add and what to subtract, and why.

7. Read a bit in the Bible, welcoming what God will say to you.

8. Write down insights throughout the day.

9. Spend time just thinking, walking, riding, or doing anything that is soothing.

10. Give yourself permission to sing, cry, laugh, talk to yourself, or speak aloud to the Lord.

11. Leave plenty of unscheduled time to do nothing at all before your DAWG day ends.

12. If you want goals, make them before you go home
    with two pages headed DO and DON'T. God
    will show you what belongs on each page.

A DAWG day will refresh you and change you in ways you cannot imagine. It will cultivate your heart and weed out the unimportant, the unnecessary, and, most important, the ungodly from your life. It will help you focus and give God room to both unfold his joyous plan in your life and set it in motion.

After a few DAWG days, you'll begin to notice that your life doesn't look quite as much like other people's lives. And as you continue, you'll likely see a whole-life transformation occur. Why? Because you will be opening your heart wide and relaxing your grip on those things that don't belong in your life. You'll be allowing God alone to set your agenda and fill your hours with his reasonable choices for you. You will finally be living out Psalm 85:8: "I will listen to what God the LORD will say; he promises peace to his people, his saints—but let them not return to folly."

It's worth noting that whatever God gives us to do he provides us the strength we need. When I don't have the strength or the time for an activity, I can be fairly sure it's one that *I* or *another person*—not God—has put into my hands. Through day-long interludes with God, my life becomes more focused, my choices more purposeful, and my spirit more joyful. Yours can too! If you doubt it, take a few moments to consider these women's stories…

JULIE'S STORY

Julie was strong, smart, and capable, but she was becoming a victim of her own strengths. She kept finding herself trapped in a "fun house" of busyness and activity that didn't seem to be going anywhere or having any lasting impact for God. When anything new came along, she would simply scrunch her schedule to fit it in. But eventually she reached the saturation point; each activity was overlapping another and each was robbing from the quality of every other. She had maxed out—and she was determined to change.

She took two days away at a quaint bed-and-breakfast inn, taking with her only her notebook, a mentor/friend, and her Bible. She walked and she prayed, and she began to listen…to agree with God…and finally to change. When she got home, she began making calls to eliminate instead of add. In a matter of weeks, her lifeboat was once more floating peacefully, and she had made room in her life for God to fill her heart and her hands. He did so quite quickly, opening the doors to a secret heart's desire: quilting. She joined a club and saw him open one door after another in the direction of her dreams.

BARBARA'S STORY

Barbara was also strong, healthy, young, and well educated. She had a lot of interests, and there wasn't much she couldn't do. So she tried most of it—all at the same time. She, too, found herself continuously busy but not entirely sure what she was accomplishing. Her activities were worthwhile and contributed greatly to her church and community. But they detracted from some of her significant relationships and from her own soul, and she felt she was on a merry-go-round, just going in endless circles. Her mind and her life were spinning.

Barbara chose to spend a night at her sister's cottage to assess her activities. She listed them and ruthlessly chopped out those that didn't have a clear and worthwhile purpose. She made more room for God, for herself, and for her significant others, and over the next several months, she finished up various commitments and projects. She now had *room* in her life.

Once her life began to open up, God began working in her heart. Barbara soon realized it had been shuttered off by her busyness. Together, she and God addressed the pain of her abortion nineteen years earlier. He took her on a three-year journey of healing. She is now working in an abortion recovery ministry that is both clearly ordained for her and richly rewarding. How did she get to this place? Simply by making room in her life for God to work.

> *"Keep your attention on this day, its charms and obligations,*
> *and forget about the yesterdays and tomorrows."*
>
> —VICTORIA MORAN

So how can you make room? Well, you could start by trading homes with a friend, as described in the previous interlude. Or you could spend a day in a library reading room or an empty church sanctuary, a Sunday school room or a retreat center or monastery. You could choose to take a long drive in your car and park beside some inspiring scenery or a refreshing body of water. Check into a motel or a B&B (I do that twice a year). Set aside a day in your own home, if you can, and don't answer the phone or turn on a computer or TV. Take a daylong bike ride or hike, talking with God all the way. Get Timothy Jones's excellent book *A Place for God,* and choose from among the destinations he recommends for a spiritual retreat.

Dress simply on your day alone with God. Underplan. Underprepare. Plan to undereat or even to fast. Give your body a chance to recreate too. Think of it as shedding unnecessary clothes. You may not even need to wear a watch. Forget responsibilities and schedules and voice mail.

This kind of time with God is a tryst for the bridegroom and his bride. He seeks a bride who loves him with abandon, who ardently desires his company alone. If you are a stranger to such solitude in the presence of God, then these interludes are a worthwhile experiment. You may actually come face to face with yourself and with God in a way that thrills your soul and heals your heart. He will never disappoint you when you turn your heart wholly to him. Your tears will be dried. Your pathway will begin to be set straight. Your desires will be aligned with his. And your gifts and passions will be regathered from the four winds where they may have been scattered for far too long.

You may not know how much good a DAWG day has done until you return home. Only then will you discover you have much more patience, an enlivened interest in life, and more energy. A DAWG day is the ultimate personal sabbath, which surely pleases the Creator who himself set the example by resting on the seventh day. He wants us to intentionally insert sabbaths into our lives and to take joy and delight in them.

Now I put DAWG days on my calendar every January so I have them to look forward to throughout the year. And when they arrive, I rejoice! I know that in a mere twenty-four hours, I will be completely refreshed.

I vividly recall a DAWG day I spent in northern Michigan—a favorite spot our family had visited for years. The little tourist home in Beulah overlooked a sparkling lake and a small beach. Life was slower and easier to manage somehow. Stores opened later and closed earlier. Dogs went to work with their masters, and sunshine was the main course of each summer day. A few hours in Beulah was like a week in other places.

A woman named Jan ran the home I was staying in, and we had become good friends. She had picked her best room for me. I remember the long lazy day and how it unfurled like a flag in a gentle breeze. I had meandered through it doing first one pleasant thing, then another. And finally, the sun began to sink in the sky, and businesses began hanging CLOSED signs on their front doors.

It was a night to remember. My favorite instrumental music drifted in magical waves around my cozy room, and I, in a chair plumped with pillows, watched night envelop day over the lake.

In those moments, I knew the supernal joy of watching Eternal God prepare his earth and his people for bed. *Could it be,* I wondered, *that sleep was the purest form of surrender?*

I just sat and watched as shadows deepened against the orange bar of sunlit water, and starlight brightened the encroaching night. Peace on earth. Goodwill to everyone. I could feel it all around. A necklace of shoreline lights began to sparkle, and only a lone fishing vessel remained on the placid, unfurrowed brow of the lake.

I remember feeling overcome—overpowered by the hypnotic stillness that hung in the air. God had spoken. "Rest." "Renew." "Surrender to the restoration prepared for you before the foundation of the world."

I remember the ecstasy of laying my head upon the shoulder of God. The songs of the night played on as I watched, and a silken strand of moonlight wove gracefully through the misty fabric of evening shadows. How kind, I thought, and how good of God to make sky jewels for my enjoyment.

The evening was a gathering of moments to treasure and to bring up in my memory time and again when life would be busier. Nightfall was a reminder of my absolute need for absolute surrender to the One who loves me with an everlasting love. He alone is the source of all lasting joy.

Holy Lord, you do have wonderful ways of manifesting your presence! Right now, dear God, I have come to this place to find you…to worship you…to put my hand in yours again. How do I get so scattered in so short a time? There's so much I want to talk with you about. Where shall I begin?

Lord, first of all I just want to be quiet and sit with you awhile. I want to shut out all the distractions that have kept me from basking in your presence. Let me simply tell you what each one is as it enters my mind, and then help me release it to you.

And now, Lord, enter my open heart even as I have entered your presence. My spirit longs for you as a wanderer in the desert yearns for water. Let me picture you walking toward me, arms outstretched, cool drink of refreshment in hand, with that pervading light of acceptance that surrounds you. I give myself over to you to be refreshed. Nothing, no one, can meet my needs like you can.

I worship you, almighty God, for there is none like you!
I worship you, great Prince of Peace, that is what I want to do!

Lord, as I give my cares to you, ask your forgiveness for all the ways in which I fall short of your standards, and worship at your footstool, I touch the hem of your garment and feel your healing power flow into me and renew me. I am refreshed from this rest in your holy presence. And I know, once again, that I do not ever walk alone.

"Far be it from me, O Lord—far be it from my heart!
to think that just any joy will make me happy
with the heavenly joy you alone offer."

—SAINT AUGUSTINE

A Word from the Author

My own journey toward a simpler, more balanced and more joyful life began entirely against my will, with a phone call from my doctor. "You have cancer, and we want to do surgery right away."

The first thing I did was cross everything off my overcrowded calendar and proceed to go into shock at all the "white space." Life has never been the same since, and it has never been so good.

I fought both the disease and the process of recovery vigorously, wanting it to hurry up and be done with, not recognizing that it was a "severe mercy," as C. S. Lewis put it in *A Grief Observed.* During my three-year recovery period, I was forced into a healthful and balanced life I would not have chosen on my own. My life so closely resembled the culture around me that I could have "written the book" on what it was to be American, female, and also Christian.

My capacities began to shrink. I could no longer do exactly what I wanted to do on any front: eating, exercising, sleeping, working, volunteering. I now knew quickly when I did too much: My own body told me. Recovering from cancer was my boot camp for balance, and I was a reluctant, greenhorn rookie.

I had loved being involved in almost everything. And I often overdid, despite the fact I had a husband and three children who should have been my first priority. The church and the culture constantly affirmed my overextension of myself. But cancer was the gift that changed my life from frantic to full.

I began to discover how much *real* life I had missed: how many sunsets and rainbows and quiet times with God I had ignored. The scenery had been a blur instead of a blessing. Not anymore. Now my days are full, but not overly so. "No" has become easy to say. Occupation and activities and family walk happily side by side; I have "enough" time and energy for each. And my ability to find a surge of joy at any given moment, instead of "tomorrow, when I'll have time," has returned. There is *now* time for the best and for the beautiful. My life is *now* a song to sing. And having once heard the music of the abundant life Christ promised me, I simply cannot do without the melody.